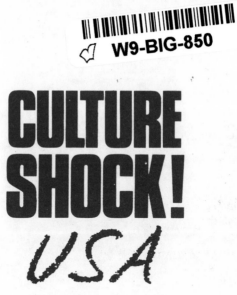

CULTURE SHOCK!

USA

Esther Wanning

TIMES BOOKS INTERNATIONAL
Singapore • Kuala Lumpur

In the same series

China
France
Indonesia
Pakistan
Thailand

Forthcoming

Britain
Sri Lanka
Malaysia
Japan
Nepal
Australia
Singapore
Philippines
Italy
Korea
Canada
India

Illustrations by TRIGG
Cover photographs by courtesy of
Cathay Pacific Airways Ltd and Tuck Loong

© 1991 Esther Wanning

This book is published by
Times Books International,
an imprint of Times Editions Pte Ltd
Times Centre, 1 New Industrial Road
Singapore 1953
2nd Floor, Wisma Hong Leong Yamaha
50 Jalan Penchala, 46050 Petaling Jaya
Selangor, Malaysia

Printed in Singapore by Chong Moh Offset Printing Pte Ltd

ISBN 981 204 193 1

To Barbara Creaturo,
who made an author out of me.

The Statue of Liberty, a present from the French, was erected in New York Harbor in 1903 to welcome immigrants to the USA. The inscription is from a poem by Emma Lazarus and reads in part:
Give me your tired, your poor,
Your huddled masses yearning to breathe free,
The wretched refuse of your teeming shore.
Send these, the homeless, tempest-tossed to me,
I lift my lamp beside the golden door!

CONTENTS

FOREWORD

Any book that attempts to generalize about culture must begin with a disclaimer. No amount of research entirely eliminates the author's own particular outlook and background. The unavoidable facts about this author: A native of Massachusetts, descended from Scottish, English, Irish, and Dutch forebears. As a child, I passed five treasured years in a small farming town in New York State, a place that clung to old-fashioned American values. As an adult, I lived for a dozen years in New York City and have spent the last 15 years in California, where I married into a Jewish family of Hungarian and Eastern European origins.

I have my grandmother, Mary Hannah Augusta Fife Emerson, to thank for early instruction in correct behavior. Her emphasis on points of etiquette left me more observant of the lapses of others than I would sometimes wish to be.

However, the fish do not have the necessary perspective for reporting on their own sea, and this book could not have been written without the help of the many immigrants I interviewed, some of whom were old friends. Their reflections make up the backbone of this book. My greatest thanks go to An-Ching Chang, Uwe Dobers, Mufeed Droubi, Ocean Epstein, Angelo Garro, Brian Gitta, Bernadette Glenn, Greg Gorel, Agneta Heijl, Lakshmi Karna, Lata Karna, Fauz Kassamali, Dorothy Kino, Fusao Kiuchi, Ashis Mukhopadhyay, Citania Tam, Mike Pham, Edda Piccini, Alice Leong Smith, and Regina Waldman.

Kathleen Wolf directed me to some rare texts (such as Judy Winn-Bell Olsen's unpublished *Little Glimpses*) and also arranged for me to meet her language classes and those of Josephine Lewis at Alemany Community College in San Francisco. These roomfuls of students from around the world produced wonderful insights.

For editorial help, earnest thanks go to Andrews Wanning, Beth Gutcheon and Robin Clements, Suzanne Mantell, Jim Churchill, and Nikki Meredith, all of whom helped save me from myself. For other kinds of help, I am grateful to Sally Taylor, Patricia Emerson Watson, Rufus Wanning, Bill Wilson, Kathy Stein, Lynn Ferrin, and Elsa and Alfred Lipsey. For generosity with photographs, Marcia Lieberman and *The Weekly Packet* of Blue Hill, Maine. For hospitality above and beyond the call of duty, the Press family of Inverness, California. My husband, Michael Lipsey, stood staunchly by, contributing moral and editorial support as the process of producing this book went on and on.

Finally, I must thank those many cultural analysts who went before me, whose books are listed in the bibliography at the end.

Esther Wanning
San Francisco, 1990

INTRODUCTION

Foreign vacationers to the United States are likely to return home delighted by our country. Its vastness and landscapes surpass expectation, the richness of an ordinary home seems astonishing, and, above all, the friendliness of the people to strangers is unforgettable. Should your sojourn here consist only of a few weeks' sightseeing, you can remain comfortably on the surface of American life and never worry about culture shock.

Culture shock is what happens when you stick around a little longer. It is the most natural – and elusive – of ailments. "If one were to offer men the choice of all the customs in the world, they would examine the whole number and end up by preferring their own," wrote the Greek historian Herodotus almost 25 centuries ago, describing culture shock. But we rarely are insightful enough to realize that it's cultural differences that separate us. We don't see our own ways of doing things as conditioned in the cradle. We see them as correct, and we conclude that the people from the other country have grave failings.

So our longer-term visitors start to complain, "These Americans are always in a hurry," and "They are so materialistic." "They aren't sincere." "The children are spoiled."

The points vary according to country of origin. Brazilians find us work-crazed, the Japanese think we are self-indulgent, the British consider us unsophisticated, and the Mexicans call us greedy. Nearly everybody considers us friendly, energetic, and fair-minded.

Our particular qualities, for better or worse, have made the country what it is today. Certain values may seem questionable to you, but if you grasp what makes Americans tick, your stay here – whether long or short – will be far more interesting and your culture shock shorter lasting.

If you have come to stay for good, it is all the more important that you try to be sympathetic to American culture. In fact, you will do best to acquire some American qualities yourself if you want to succeed. Furthermore, you don't want to end up in one of those enclaves of foreigners which nourish themselves on disdain for America – while their own children are becoming more and more American. (This is not the same thing as valuing your own customs and culture, a blameless idea.)

To shed light on American culture is only half the reason for this book. The other half is to acquaint you with the specific customs and habits of the American people. It is in the small differences that most misunderstandings occur. For instance, if you offer a limp handshake to an American while looking downwards, the American will not imagine that you are behaving very politely by your own rules; instead he will assume that you are a lackluster kind of person.

"When in Rome, do as the Romans do" is a useful adage for both immigrants and short-term visitors, but to follow it you must know what they do. This book attempts to show what Americans do in the areas of life in which you are most apt to encounter them. You do not need to adopt these customs as your own, but if you know what they are, you will find your encounters with Americans both more fruitful and more frequent.

Your Welcome

Although you can expect to find Americans welcoming and friendly, this is not altogether an easy country for foreigners to travel in. Very few Americans have any command of a foreign language, and not many have any sense of how differently things are done in other places. If something baffles you, speak up. We are likely to think you know more than you do.

On the other hand, the way of the foreigner is made easier because this is a "low-context" culture, which means that we don't assume a great deal in our conversation. Unlike the high-context

Japanese, whose words must be interpreted through understanding of the culture, we Americans are straightforward. Yes means yes, and no means no.

Furthermore, our protocol is not strict. In social situations, you needn't be overly concerned about correct behavior, and if you eat with the wrong fork or wear blue jeans to a cocktail party, few people will be offended. There are few taboos and not many formalities expected of anyone. The rules of behavior are vague even for us.

The drawback to this looseness is that you can't look forward to mastering every situation through learning precise forms. To a larger extent than in most cultures, you're on your own, trying to fit in but having to write your own script. It's like the difference between the waltz and disco dancing. For disco dancing, you have to figure out your own moves, but if you get too original, you won't find partners. So it is in our social interactions. You're allowed wide latitude, but there are limits.

After reading this book, you should know where those limits lie. Meanwhile, smile – as Americans constantly do – and don't worry. "In the end," as an Indian friend said after enumerating her complaints about Americans, "people are really more alike than different." If you learn the native customs, you will go beyond the smaller differences and on to the big things that we all have in common.

Chapter One

AMERICAN VALUES

Like peoples everywhere, Americans don't think of themselves as having American values. We simply imagine that the qualities we hold dear are those that matter to all mankind.

In this we are mistaken. American values are uncommon. This becomes quickly clear when an American advisor launches a project in an underdeveloped country. The American, who plans to bring prosperity to the natives, ends up in despair because nothing gets done. He cannot imagine that there are societies where getting things done isn't top priority. He is baffled to discover people who do not aspire to change their standards of living. He cannot understand individuals who are not eager to change their status in society. He goes home in defeat, thanking God that he is an American.

What he does not understand is that American values could only have been forged in a new country full of opportunity. We are a nation almost entirely of immigrants, steeped in the belief that anyone with talent can get ahead.

American culture is commonly dated from the first permanent English settlement of 1607; from that point we see our history as a record of progress: from wilderness to jet planes in a few centuries. We conquered the original inhabitants, overthrew the English rulers, cleared the forests, opened the West, built skyscrapers, won the World Wars and extended the comfortable life to the masses. We achieved all this – as we see it – because of dynamic individuals who never stopped seeking a better way.

Equality

More than anything else, our values have been shaped by the fact that this has been a nation in which ambition could be rewarded. That all people should have an equal chance at success remains a sacred belief.

It has been opportunity, rather than democracy, that has given America its name as the Land of the Free. Were resources scarce and possibilities limited, people would only be free to go nowhere, and equality would have had a very different meaning. Our equality is the equality of opportunity. "Any man's son may become the equal of any other man's son," wrote Fanny Trollope in 1831, "and the consciousness of this is certainly a spur to exertion."

When the country was founded, the population was small and the resources were vast; those both aggressive and lucky could go far. In 1782, a Frenchman, St. John de Crevecoeur, noted that it was in going from a servant to a master that a man became an American. Actually, many people through the years remained downtrodden, but there have been enough examples of upward mobility to keep the myth of equality alive. Democracy could promise visible fruits. Everybody might not win, but everybody (so goes the myth) was eligible to get out on the racecourse. Family and connections were not required. Effort and brains and imagination were.

Because the country's natural resources seemed endless, Americans developed an economics of abundance. We do not see our personal wealth as having been gained at the expense of others, as most of the world does. Instead, we think of the rich as creating opportunities and jobs for others. We are very frank about liking rich people and wanting to be rich ourselves.

The American system contributed the sense that everybody played by the same rules. The government's job was to keep the course equal, to protect the rights of the individual. When people at least believe that they have a chance, it seems worthwhile to try to advance themselves – and when they fail, to try again. If, on the contrary, they feel that only those in favored positions can succeed, they are not inspired to make an effort. (The belief in this fairness was often naïve, but it kept people trying.) Despite the fact that it obviously is not so, we like to think that anyone can become President of the United States – regardless of family, wealth, or background.

Future Outlook

Americans are profoundly future-oriented. Whereas other societies look to the past for guidance, we cast our nets forward. We have a nearly exclusive respect for the future and what it will bring.

It's the belief in a brighter future that gives us our optimism. Whereas most peoples see their histories as cycles of good times and bad, we see ours as one of constant improvement. We trust that we have the power to affect the course of events. We do not believe that bad things are God's will, things to be endured.

Even these days, when not all progress seems positive (nuclear weapons, air pollution, unemployment, loss of world power, etc.), the belief remains that for every problem there is a rational solution. If it's ourselves we must change, we do so.

13

The notion that the present can always be improved accounts for Americans being in such a hurry. The contemplative man accepts the world as it is; the active man changes it. It is change that Americans believe in. Consequently, to say that somebody is "very energetic" (no matter in what cause) is one of our highest compliments.

Future Shock

Because change comes so thick and fast, the American has been called "the constantly jumping man." The last two decades have been particularly fast-paced, in gadgetry as well as in mores. Just in the last few years, fax machines, cellular phones, computerized burglar alarms, microwave ovens, and video cassette recorders have become commonplace.

Alvin Toffler in his popular book, *Future Shock*, made the claim that all Americans are living in a state of shock due to the increasing tempo of change in our lives. Future shock, he says, is worse than culture shock because there is no resolution. The only resource is to become more adaptable than ever before, leading to a loss of identity.

Others would argue that all these changes are superficial, and American life continues with the family around the turkey at Thanksgiving, with morals and outlook intact. But at the very least, the acquisition and care of new products explains where a lot of an American's leisure time goes.

Independence

Cowboys never were a large part of the population, and they're very scarce now, but in many ways they characterize the American ideal – self-reliant, tough, risk-taking, and masculine. The cowboy stands alone, pitting himself against the elements. His strongest tie is to his horse.

In many countries, people cannot conceive of themselves apart from the family or group they belong to; their loyalty is to the group

Photo: Marcia Lieberman

Children are encouraged to do things for themselves at a young age.

and their achievements are for the group. In America, instead, self-reliance is the fundamental virtue. Each person is a solo operation, and independence is considered the birthright of every child. Our highest aspiration is self-fulfillment, and it's only the unencumbered person who can become his true self. Many decisions that would be made by the group in other cultures are made by the individual here.

Newcomers, especially those from tightly knit families, are frequently aghast to discover that American children quite regularly leave home – with their parents' blessings – at the age of 18. From then on, they will make most of their own decisions without their parents' help, having already been quite independent during their teenage years. Should they linger too long under the parental roof they will cause anxiety. The child's job is to go out into the world and succeed. The job of the parents is to give the children every opportunity while they are growing up and then get out of their way.

Realistically, there are many ways in which families can and do help their grown children, but they will try to make light of their assistance. Children are not to be burdened with a sense of obligation.

Asian families, who are often successful in acquiring real estate in the United States, are surprised to discover that American parents are not expected to contribute to the down payment on a house for their married children. Although this leaves the children free of obligation to them, it also – especially in these times of high real estate prices – leaves many bereft of any hope of owning a house.

Many of the aspects of American life that seem most baffling to foreigners make sense in light of the freedom principle. Aged parents as well as children remain independent. If you want to be a salmon fisherman in Alaska, you go. You don't have to stay home to take care of your elders. In fact, sticking around your home town could suggest a lack of backbone, a failure of imagination and courage. American psychiatrists are quick to conclude that their patients' problems stem from "inadequate separation" from parents.

The individual comes first. We do not consider this selfish. A person serves society by living up to his potential. The classic American hero is someone who succeeded on his own, pulling himself up by his own bootstraps. The finest American literature extols the rebel: *Huckleberry Finn*, *Moby Dick*, *Walden*. "I Did It My Way," sang Frank Sinatra in a classic popular song.

Authority

It will not come as a surprise that a society that admires independence and progress does not have an automatic respect for authority. What deference people in authority do command is based on their actual powers rather than on their age, wisdom, or dignity. Old people are often seen as behind the times. It's the young who are expected to have some special insight into the modern world.

After all, it was by overthrowing the King of England that the United States was born, and suspicion of authority has remained a pillar of American life. This attitude has helped establish the USA as the birthplace of innovations that have changed the world. If a better way of doing something comes along, we unsentimentally jettison the old way. But we also jettison people. In a society that changes as fast as ours, experience simply does not have the value that it does in traditional societies.

Land of the Too-Free

"I think one person should end where the other begins," said one immigrant to the United States. Many foreigners agree that American freedom is excessive. Americans tend to leap to the conclusion that any limitation on their rights is an attack on the American way of life. Out on the frontier you could do anything you wanted for the simple reason that nobody was around to notice. (The true frontiersman picked up stakes and moved as soon as he could smell his neighbor's smoke.)

In urban life, there are plenty of ways to bother the neighbors, from shooting them to scrawling graffiti on their buildings. While nobody is allowed to do such things, the criminal gets the benefit of the doubt; under our legal system, he is innocent until proven guilty. We look for psychological reasons for anti-social behavior; there are even people who defend graffiti on the grounds that it is a form of self-expression.

Businesses, also, resist regulation. It has taken a long time to convince the public that free enterprise does not mean that a company should be free to pollute the air, foul the rivers, and destroy the forests. Such problems, of course, are not unique to this society.

The Puritan Tradition

Although we have gone from a rural society to an urban one, many American values remain the traditional ones established by the European settlers in the 17th century.

The Puritans, a stern Christian sect, were among the first and most lasting settlers. Their values were well-suited to survival in a strange new world: self-reliance, hard work, frugal living, and the guidance of the individual conscience.

Furthermore, the Puritans considered earthly success a sign of God's favor and saw no conflict between making money and entering the kingdom of heaven. Americans continue to have few ideas about the holiness of poverty. On the contrary, there is an undercurrent of feeling that people get what they deserve. (For that reason, this is a difficult country in which to be handicapped as well as in which to be poor.)

The Puritans would not have smiled on the conspicuous consumption of today, but they would have admired the unrelenting effort that goes into the acquisition of goods. Americans have much greater respect for businessmen than most other peoples do. An Englishman who has made enough money may well be happy to retire to his country home. The American only wants to go on making more money, driven as much by the Puritan work ethic (often called "the Protestant work ethic") as by the desire for more money.

The "Puritan values" still referred to today usually refer to a prudishness towards sex and enjoyment. Although the Puritans were not actually against good times, they did feel that man was basically sinful, and spontaneity revealed the inner wickedness. Today, to call someone "Puritanical" is generally not meant as a compliment, as it suggests that he or she is strait-laced and no fun.

Efficiency: Time Is Money

If there is anything that warms the American heart, it's efficiency. Henry Ford was long regarded as a hero for, of all things, inventing the assembly line. The assembly line reduced workers to cogs of machinery and made their jobs unutterably boring, but it produced goods fast.

"Time is money," we say. Nothing is more American than the supermarket. Food is prepackaged, and shopping is impersonal, but the efficiency of the operation produces lower prices and less shopping time. The food's lack of tastiness has not created much customer resistance.

Fast-food operations calculate sharply ways of saving a few seconds in the time each customer must wait. The customer will choose the one that can serve his hamburger and Coke in 60, rather than 90, seconds.

We show little forbearance if our time is wasted. A chatty bank teller whose line is moving slowly will cause great dismay. The people waiting in line are not inclined to chat. The important business while waiting is to be ready to move forward instantly when the line

"Cloverleafs" such as this make highway travel very fast, but you'd better know which signs to follow or you can get horribly lost.

19

does, and to be prepared to dispatch one's business in the least amount of time possible. If you should reach the head of the bank line before you remember to make out a deposit slip, and the whole line must wait while you do so, you will be looked on with disfavor.

Time Waits for No Man

According to anthropologist Edward T. Hall, we are a monochronic culture, meaning we operate according to schedules, doing one thing at a time. Sticking to the schedule is more important than the human interruptions to it. When the bell rings, the class is over, no matter how interesting the discussion at that moment.

In a polychronic culture, on the other hand, many things are happening at once. It doesn't matter if you're late for an appointment because you're only going to join the ongoing flow of business, none more pressing than the personal. Even if not much at all is happening, nobody cares. Life is not destination bound as it is with us.

There are Asian countries at least as efficient as the USA, but vast parts of the world cannot conceive of our concept of time. Time is all-important to us. We think of ourselves as people who are going places. Tomorrow is not going to be like today. Tomorrow we'd like to be "a ways" down the road, and speed is going to get us there, not standing around chatting.

Consequently, we have come to see only practical and profitable activity as truly valuable. "How has so spartan a philosophy descended on an age that hoped to make machines do all the useful work while man enjoyed his leisure?" asked Walter Kerr in his book, *The Decline of Pleasure*.

A good question. An American often lacks the capacity to enjoy his achievements. We find more satisfaction in acquiring the trappings of the leisure life than in leisure itself. Activity – rather than family or community – gives us our identities, and very few people are able to rest on their laurels. The Puritan values still dominate.

The No-Status Society

In a status society, people learn their places and gain some dignity and security from having a place in the social order. Americans, however, are taught not to recognize their places and to constantly assert themselves. This can manifest itself in positive ways – hard work, clever ideas – but also in ongoing dissatisfaction.

As an American is always striving to change his lot, he never fully identifies with any group. We have no expressions such as in China where "the fat pig gets slaughtered," or in Japan, where "the nail that sticks out gets hammered down." Here, everybody is trying to stick out, which limits closeness between people. We say, "It's the squeaky wheel that gets the grease." According to Alan Roland, author of *In Search of Self in India and Japan*, in the United States "a militant individualism has been combined with enormous social mobility," leaving very little group identity.

Roland psychoanalyzed Americans, Indians, and Japanese and discovered that the two Asian cultures had no concept of the strong inner separation from others that is characteristic of Americans. Because our society is so competitive, we feel in the end that we can only rely on ourselves.

This freedom from the group has enabled the American to become "Economic Man" – one directed almost purely by the profit motive, mobile and unencumbered by family or community obligations. It's a personality type well suited to national development, but one that leads to identity problems for the individual himself.

"Identity is the number one national problem here," writes Eva Hoffman, the Polish-born author of *Lost in Translation*. "Many of my American friends feel they don't have enough of it. They often feel worthless or they don't know how they feel."

But to someone who feels oppressed in another culture, American life can look wonderful. "Americans have a blank check, on which they can write anything they want," concluded one foreigner after ten years here.

Discontent

If you can never be content with your station, you are never satisfied. The idea of equality is an inspiration, but people can be tricked by it. No success is good enough. Not everybody can reach the top, and those who don't blame themselves.

A status society teaches that every place is worthy; in ours none is. The fear of failure in itself arouses widespread insecurity. Failure in this society is more shameful than poverty in a status society because failure is assumed to be a person's own fault.

The Status Seekers

"I just wanted to find a place where I would be accepted," said an East German who is happily settled in San Francisco. He is delighted that you don't have to be a doctor to be treated with respect and that people don't care who your father is. But the myth of equality should not fool anyone into thinking that America doesn't have a class system.

What makes our class system different from most is its fluidity; penetration at most levels is possible for nearly anyone with enough money. Equipped with the money, one can acquire the taste, style, and ideas that mark each class and launch a quick ascent of the social ladder.

There do exist a few clubs, societies, and debutante balls which require old money for entry. People whose families were among the early arrivals in America like to have it known, but in point of fact, such lineage doesn't mean much (politicians prefer to advertise their humble beginnings), and one's level in society can be – like so many other things in American life – determined by one's own efforts. (Of course, few people actually do go from the bottom to the top. Most of the jockeying around is for levels in the middle class.) One must speak correct English to progress upward socially, but correct English is not nearly as hard to learn as correct Japanese.

There are certain accents that will take you further than others, but few leave a person out of the running altogether.

Money is the key to social position, and it is nearly impossible to be upper class without it (with the possible exception of Southern aristocrats). Thus the seriousness of money. If I make a lot of money, I can drive a Mercedes, buy a big house, and join a country club. I will be accepted, not just because I have the money, but because the money proves that I have performed in society at a high level. If I am truly socially ambitious, and have enough money to give large amounts to prestigious charities, I can hire a promoter who will guide me in an assault on high society.

Foreigners find Americans terribly materialistic, but they often fail to understand the important symbolic value of money. Money demonstrates success and shows the world that I have lived up to my promise.

Conformity

To an American, what the world thinks of him is extremely important. Only through the eyes of others can success have significance. The theory of culture analyst David Riesman (author of *The Lonely Crowd*) is that Americans are no longer primarily governed by inner values handed down through generations. Instead, he thinks Americans have become outer-directed people – guided not by their own consciences but by the opinions of others. To be liked is crucial.

Although individualism is central in America – in the sense that the self comes first – Americans are not individualists. Actually, persons in status societies who are secure in their niches are allowed more eccentricity than Americans, who rely heavily on signals that other people like them. In America, popularity is a sign of success and terribly important. Nobody can have too many friends – as long as they don't take up too much of their valuable time.

The Contradictions

The alert visitor will quickly note much that seems contradictory in American life. Freedom of the press has not produced a well-informed public. Despite our wealth, we have people sleeping in the streets. Americans are friendly, but neighbors don't stop to chat. Supplied by the world's richest farmlands, America's cuisine leaves much to be desired.

The social commentator Paul Goodman aptly wrote, "America has a high standard of living of low average quality." Despite the luxuries and conveniences Americans enjoy, our lives are not very elegant. Equality has a way of leading to mediocrity. When half the population goes to college, one cannot expect the colleges to maintain the same standards as in countries where only the elite attend. Television shows are expected to appeal to the lowest common denominator. Mass produced goods are not finely crafted.

Not all contradictions are reconcilable. We are anti-royalist but fascinated by royalty. We are suspicious of government but re-elect incumbents over and over. We are a religious people (compared to other westernized societies) but many of our much-revered founding fathers were not.

Expect also to find innumerable exceptions to any of these claims about American life. Generalizations should not be used to pigeonhole individuals. Just as not every Japanese is hardworking and deferential to superiors, nor every Chinese devoted to family, not every American is ambitious or patriotic – or even unsophisticated.

Chapter Two

AMERICAN ORIGINS

The only indigenous people here are the Indians (now often called "Native Americans"). The rest of us spring from families who immigrated to this country within recent history.

Among whites, the English were the earliest arrivals, settling the first permanent colony in 1607. They were soon followed by Spanish, Dutch, French, Scottish, Irish, and German settlers. In the 19th century, great numbers of Irish and Chinese immigrated, escaping famines at home. Thereafter, there were waves of Scandinavians, Italians, Russians, Jews, and Greeks. Most of these people arrived poor and stayed poor; the high levels of immigration kept wages minimal. In 1922, Congress set quotas, repealed in 1943, that favored Anglo-Saxons and virtually barred Asians and Africans.

The ancestors of Black Americans were brought here forcibly from Africa as slaves. Slave-trading was outlawed after 1807 and therefore the families of Blacks have been here longer than most. The slaves were freed by the Civil War, which ended in 1865.

Immigrants from Mexico, Cuba, Central America, and Asia now predominate, once again changing the ethnic make-up of the country. The number of illegal immigrants slipping in from south of the border add to a large, low-paid labor pool.

Choice Grain

It is an axiom among Americans that we are an exceptional people because our forebears were those with the pluck to abandon their native lands and start anew here. As early as 1668, a William Stoughton wrote that God "sifted a whole nation [England] that he might send choice grain over into this wilderness."

The American humorist H.L. Mencken argued instead that "the majority of non-Anglo-Saxon immigrants since the revolution, like the majority of Anglo-Saxon immigrants before the revolution, have been, not the superior men of their native lands, but the botched and unfit." It was Mencken's view that it was so easy to get ahead in America because the competition was third-rate.

Mencken's school of thought, however, has no following. Americans generally consider themselves to be superior to all other peoples, an attitude often annoying to foreigners.

Early Days

When Christopher Columbus, celebrated as the discoverer of America, landed in the West Indies in 1492, he found a generous and friendly people whom he called Indians (because he thought he had discovered the westward route to India). He killed some, captured others, and enslaved still more to mine for gold.

When the English settlers arrived in the 17th century, many Indians naïvely thought there could be room for both themselves and the Europeans; the Indians did not understand the concept of private property that drove the newcomers. They also lacked European firepower, and when driven to defend their land, their bows and arrows proved no match for guns.

By various means, the whites massacred the Indians throughout the first two hundred years of their occupation, until the Indian population was reduced to a fifth of its original size and pushed onto reservations in the infertile West. The last major battle wasn't fought until 1890, but it was clear much earlier that the Land of the Braves had passed into European hands.

American culture acquired a few agricultural tips and some place names from the Indians, but little else. Our language, institutions, and religion came directly from Europe. For many years so did the livestock, fine clothes and furniture, literature and music.

The Declaration of Independence

Wars between European nations had left the English ruling northeastern America, but the colonists chafed against English rule and taxation. In 1776, they rebelled. In the famous Declaration of Independence ("We hold these truths to be self-evident, that all men are created equal; that they are endowed by their Creator with certain unalienable rights; that among these, are life, liberty, and the pursuit of happiness"), the colonists declared themselves an independent nation. Five years of fighting ensued – the War of Independence – at the end of which the British surrendered and went home, and the original thirteen colonies became a free nation, the United States of America.

The United States Constitution

In 1789, the American government was formally established

according to the United States Constitution, which includes the Bill of Rights – in which individual rights are upheld against those of the government. The Constitution is vastly quoted in American life, most frequently those parts that deal with freedom of religion, free speech, freedom of assembly, and freedom of the press.

It is because of these Constitutional rights that prayer is not allowed in the schools; that newspapers may criticize the government; that the police may not search your home without a warrant; and that any group may form a political party. The determination of Constitutional rights lies with the Supreme Court, which decides how the Constitution relates to specific cases.

The system of government outlined in the Constitution derived from English traditions – limitation of executive power, bicameral legislature, trial by jury, and protection of individual rights. Although one may object that the system has best served the interests of the landowners who created it, it has at least provided a government of unusual stability.

States' Rights

Many rights and responsibilities were reserved for individual states, which causes confusion for visiting foreigners. Many laws (such as the laws regarding divorce, drinking, wages, guns, education, and driving) vary from state to state. Corporations establish their headquarters in a particular state and then must follow the laws of that state. Each state has its own school system and its own system of taxation.

One Creed/One Nation

The ideal of democracy/equality/freedom served an important purpose as the country grew older. As a nation, America was singularly bereft of unifying concepts. Whereas most peoples are unified by race, language, culture, traditions, and history, America's immigrant population had little in common other than the initiative to get here. In the days when communication was slow, the country was too big for centralized government. Instead, democracy became the faith, the unifying theme, of the new nation. America may be the only country in the world founded on a creed.

During the first half of the 19th century, the doctrine of equal rights was developed to mythical proportions. A.A. Bennet wrote in 1827, "We may look forward to the period when the spark kindled in America shall spread and spread, till the whole earth be illumined by its light." Individual liberty, in the American mind, became synonymous with America, and Americans consider themselves the world's freest people.

Americans remain extremely proud of their democratic political system. Everyone over 18 qualifies to vote, and we generally feel that ours is a government ruled by the people. There are two major political parties – the Democrats and the Republicans – which make nearly every election a contest. Despite an increasing number of skeptics who maintain that both parties represent special interests, rather than the people, no notable third party has emerged. Foreigners often find Americans naïve about politics and ignorant of foreign affairs. Do not expect that Americans will know anything about your country's government, wherever it is.

But Some Weren't So Equal

In reality, Constitutional rights have been unevenly distributed throughout our history. Each immigrant group has been subjected to discrimination; the Chinese in particular suffered from laws that once prohibited Chinese land ownership, school attendance, marriage with whites, and other rights. Blacks have had a long and unique history of discrimination.

Women were not allowed to vote until 1920, and it is only in the last twenty years that discriminatory laws against women have been struck down. Today, all discrimination according to race, color, sex, or creed is illegal, but it continues in subtle forms.

Furthermore, no one could seriously think that anyone who grows up poor, lives in a bad neighborhood, and attends an inferior school has an opportunity equal to that of someone more favored. However, even in these cases, the possibility of success exists; those exceptional persons who do overcome such a background can rise to any level.

Americans have one shining asset, which is that at least philosophically we are against prejudice. Most Americans do not accept the idea that some people are born inferior to others, and it is not socially acceptable to make slighting statements about people on the basis of their race. (However, people are not as delicate about references to nationality, and jokes about the Polish, the Irish, the Chinese, the Scottish, etc., are widespread.) To dislike people because of their color is considered ignorant and stupid, and no responsible public speaker makes outright racist statements. We may not have achieved equality, but at least we aspire to it, which is more than many nations can claim.

The foreigners interviewed for this book (from all parts of the world) held that racism has not been a big problem for them. Today there are many more women, Blacks, Hispanics, and other ethnic groups in government than in years past; it's the economic pie that has not been so readily shared. While immigrants are free to make their fortunes in whatever niche they can find – often in the newer industries – the large, old corporations don't have much diversity at the top.

Black Americans

The lot of Blacks has been the most difficult of any American group. Until the Civil War, they lived under one of the most brutalizing versions of slavery in history. Afterwards, they began their lives as free people without property, skills, education, or civil rights, in a land in which they were widely regarded as inferior.

In the Old South (the Southeast) especially, where most of them lived, Blacks were segregated. They were not allowed to eat in white restaurants, stay in white hotels, or use white bathrooms. Schools, parks, and swimming pools were all segregated. The worst jobs were reserved for Blacks. It was not until 1955 when a tired Black woman, Rosa Parks, refused to give up a seat on the bus to a white man, that the civil rights movement succeeded in integrating public facilities. In 1964, an omnibus Civil Rights Bill was passed by Congress, banning public segregation.

Blacks also fought a long struggle in the North against unofficial segregation, which was not so blatant as in the South, but has proven perhaps even more persistent. Blacks lived in separate neighborhoods and were the last hired and first fired. Since the civil rights movement, there has been a court-mandated effort to right some of the wrongs of the past through the hiring and career advancement of Blacks.

Nonetheless, the problems of Blacks have not been easily solved. While many Blacks are educated and of the middle class, a minority make up the Black "underclass" – a group that has slipped out of mainstream society altogether into one in which the problems of unemployment, crime, drugs, and poverty are overwhelming.

Homosexuals

Homosexuals were disdained in America for many years and only recently has public opinion changed. Thanks largely to a civil rights movement similar to that of Blacks and women, the law has recognized that to discriminate against someone because of "sexual preference" is as bad as discriminating on the basis of color. It has helped that evidence now suggests that sexual preference is inborn and not a perverse refusal to accept society's mores.

Many gays and lesbians (homosexual men and women) still feel that prejudice requires them to conceal their homosexuality. Nonetheless, the progress towards equal rights in the past twenty years has been tremendous, and there are now openly gay and lesbian people in police departments and even in the US Congress. Gays have particularly won admiration by their fortitude and activism in the face of the AIDS crisis. It is notable how many of the men who died have, even at young ages, been prominent in their fields.

The Rise of the USA

The United States, despite its burgeoning wealth, was not of importance to the world at large until this century. Foreigners often considered Americans ignorant, uncultured, and unsophisticated. Before modern communications, Americans were too far from the European capitals to follow their fashions and too busy working the land to care about them.

After the two World Wars of the century, however, the USA could no longer be regarded as a backwater. Whatever our cultural deficits, our farms provided food for the world, and our factories exported much of the world's manufactured goods. American jazz and American movies had already stamped the USA onto world consciousness. Today, our symphonies, ballets, and opera companies rank with the world's finest.

Americans have been shocked that we have recently become a nation that imports more goods than it exports. We are not a histori-cally minded people and had not imagined that our reign as the world's strongest and richest nation could be threatened. Our confi-dence in ourselves is shaken.

The Vietnam War

The Vietnam War, which engaged American troops from 1964 to 1973, caused much conflict between Americans. It gave rise to the largest anti-war movement the country had ever known; there was acute division in the country between those who did and did not support the war. At the end, despite the deaths of 50,000 Americans and the dropping of seven million tons of bombs, America withdrew in defeat. There is still bitterness in the country over the war, particularly on the part of Vietnam veterans, who feel betrayed both by the government that sent them to war and by the populace which treated them with contempt when they came home.

The Sixties

The Vietnam War gave rise to a rebellious generation. Students led the anti-war movement and from questioning the government's Vietnam policy went on to question the entire history of the United States as it had been represented in their history books. The civil rights movement had been a precursor of the anti-war movement, and the anti-war movement led in its turn to support of women's rights, Indian rights, and farm workers' rights – among others.

Society had never paid so much attention to young people before, and the anti-establishment youth dreamed of overthrowing the old power structure and establishing a new and just one. A broad spectrum of young people – who became known as "hippies" – experimented with communal living, sexual freedom, and drugs, while proclaiming the power of love. Long hair and imaginative clothes distinguished hippies from "straights." Rock music provided the theme songs.

However, the establishment hardly stumbled, and by the late seventies the aging young rebels found it politic to join society as it was. Society had certainly changed – for economic as well as political reasons. The affluence of the sixties was over. Many more women held jobs than ever before. In some respects the appearance of egalitarianism was more pronounced. Many social rituals were out, dress was more casual, discrimination less blatant. But the inequities of wealth and privilege remained; some of the sixties' generation went on to fight for environmental causes, while others turned inward to focus on personal self-fulfillment.

Famous Names of History

The most substantial American heroes rose to acclaim during the American Revolution and are known as "the founding fathers."

George Washington, a rich Virginia farmer who stands alone as the father of our country, commanded the army during the Revolution and became our first president. **Benjamin Franklin**, inventor and writer, was ambassador to France during and after the Revolution. A self-made man, the story of his rise to fame is particularly dear to American hearts. He produced many aphorisms consistent with Puritan ethics, such as "Early to bed, early to rise, makes a man healthy, wealthy and wise." **John Adams**, hard-working revolutionary, became the second president. **Thomas Jefferson** wrote the Declaration of Independence and was the third US president. **Abraham Lincoln**, president during the Civil War and credited with saving the Union, is the only name in subsequent US history that shines as brightly as those in the Revolutionary pantheon.

Other heroes are not quite as firmly rooted in the country's mythology as the aforementioned. **Susan B. Anthony** was in the forefront of the women's rights movement in the 19th century. **Harriet Tubman**, who escaped from slavery herself, led hundreds of other slaves north to freedom. President **Franklin Roosevelt** lifted the country out of the depression and put restrictions on American business. **Martin Luther King**, a black preacher and moral leader assassinated in 1968, led the civil rights movement through its darkest as well as its finest hours. **John F. Kennedy**, president from 1961 to 1963, was assassinated before achieving very much, but his youthful promise still holds the public imagination.

Any list of heroes could go on and on, but the above are a few of the names you are most apt to come across on schools, streets, and statues. According to the 1990 *World Almanac* (a valuable book for all kinds of information), the people Americans currently venerate are sports and entertainment stars – very few of whom are of any lasting consequence.

— Chapter Three —

VARIETIES OF AMERICAN LIFE

"How can you generalize about America when there are so many regional differences?" people have asked me. Americans tend to see most of our customs as normal human behavior and the few elements that vary as the cultural part. In fact, the similarities in customs across the land, big as it is, are vastly greater than the differences.

It is the culture of the white, middle class that is reflected in this book because theirs are the values and practices that shape America. Although many of our citizens are neither white nor middle class, most nonetheless subscribe to the majority outlook. Even people born elsewhere begin to change their ways after a few years' exposure. "I knew I was becoming American," says an Iranian, "when I started wanting to have time to myself."

Americans like to roam. Some retired people spend many months of the year living in their recreational vehicles, traveling from campground to campground, constantly socializing with different people.

Regional Differences

Regional differences, such as they are, are most notable in the South. Family counts for more there, and money less. Time is a little slower, hospitality a bit fuller, the work ethic slightly less full-blown. The South lost a war that the North won (the Civil War or War Between the States), which has given the white Southerner a heritage of failure and defeat that Northerners are exempt from.

Yet the South does not feel like a foreign place. Airports are identical, pay phones operate as expected, and department stores display the same labels. The same hotel and fast food chains thrive all over the country. In the commercial centers, where international businessmen gather, only the hot weather may indicate southern-ness. Anyone looking for regional variety should abandon the cities and explore small towns. Throughout the USA, there are rural communities where the values described in this book appear subordinate to family ties and tradition.

Southerners were once considered to be more racist than Northerners, but this is no longer the case. Even if it were, their racism is unlikely to extend to Asians whose numbers are small in the South. Nobody of any race is likely to encounter face-to-face rudeness. On the contrary, visitors may be particularly taken by the warmth and politeness of Southerners. However, warns a disaffected Southerner, "Don't believe everything they say."

Southerners tend to be effusive and to distrust quiet people. "It's better to babble than to be quiet in the South," says one Southerner. There's an aggressiveness in personal relations. At the same time, social circles in some cities may be closed to all newcomers – American and foreign alike – and life in the South can prove lonely for those without secure contacts.

New Englanders (in the Northeast) are quite the opposite of Southerners. They are supposedly reserved and quiet, more apt to speak in monosyllables than to babble. They are traditionalists, preferring the old to the new. They make no promises they cannot keep. They are slow to accept newcomers but will in time should the newcomers prove reliable. The foreigner living in New England needs only patience. Friendships once developed are lasting.

New Yorkers (which means residents of New York City) are in a category by themselves, with a reputation for being impatient, fast-talking, and rude. Nowhere else in the country is it necessary to put one's head down and elbows out to jam onto a subway or bus. Money talks particularly loudly in New York. Do not waste your time being offended by the rudeness of New Yorkers. Try, instead, to appreciate their wit, which New Yorkers have in abundance. Like many big cities, New York can be a lonely place, with the consequence that friends become very close.

Midwesterners are credited with being plain-speaking, casual, and conservative. One thinks of Midwesterners as unglamorous, but genuine. Midwesterners don't like "phonies" so in the Midwest we can all relax and be ourselves.

Californians, on the contrary, are expected to be trendy, superficial, and empty-headed. The beautiful blondes and the Hollywood money are concentrated in the southern part of the state. Californians pride themselves on open-mindedness and as the state is home to a vast mix of peoples, you should find ready acceptance wherever you're from.

Whatever grains of truth there might be in these stereotypes, you may have to work pretty hard to observe any of these differences. New England is full of chatty, emotional people and the South has its share of cold and quiet ones. Americans are just too mobile for regional differences to live up to their reputations.

Accents

The most notable differences in regions are in the accents. Northerners make fun of the slow Southern speech with its drawn-out vowels, and Southerners think the fast, clipped speech of Northerners sounds rude. A Western accent is an amalgam of many and not easily placed. Then there are numerous localized accents – those from Maine, Boston, and Brooklyn are all distinctive. Yet the vocabularies vary little, and few of these accents are difficult to understand for anyone who speaks fluent English. A large number of the people in every region speak without a trace of the local accent.

Food

Food, too, has a few local distinctions. You must go to the South to find hominy grits (a form of corn). New York City, heavily under the influence of the Jewish deli, serves up a vast number of hot pastrami (smoked and seasoned beef) sandwiches. You won't get many crawfish outside of Louisiana. But 90% of the dishes on any menu in the country are the same everywhere. Freezing, storage, and growing techniques have seen to it that if Americans like something, they can have it wherever they go.

Ethnic Groups

Cultural differences between ethnic groups are probably greater than regional differences. Many American Blacks have retained a separate culture with distinctive language and strong ties to the extended family. Several French writers have noted that the conversational style of Blacks, with its lively repartee, is closer to the French manner than the more plodding delivery of the white American.

Indian (Native American) tribes pride themselves on having rejected the grasping ways of the European settlers. Some Indians, living on reservations, continue to speak their own language, practice their own religion and ceremonies, and follow customs extremely foreign to those of white people. That they have continued to do so despite several centuries' efforts of missionaries and government first to annihilate and then to assimilate them, is a testament to the strength of Indian culture.

Scattered about in obscure pockets of land, most notably in the South, are traditional white communities where a great deal of what is said in this book would not apply. Here and there, religious groups live communally in defiance of the American passion for

39

private property. Unless you are an anthropologist, you are unlikely to meet any of these groups.

Less obscure are large urban communities of Chinese, Japanese, Irish, Poles, Russians, Vietnamese, Italians, Mexicans, etc. In towns and cities you can also find enclaves of Scandinavians, Hungarians, Germans, Laotians, and scores of other nationalities. Each group, to a certain extent, manages to retain aspects of their native cuisines, holidays, and habits.

Again, my interlocutors ask, how are you going to write about all this? The answer is that I am not. Above and beyond all the ethnic variety, there is an overwhelmingly dominant American Way of Life that I think it fair to generalize upon.

Despite its size, this is not as diverse a country as we sometimes like to think. We have institutions and businesses that impose uniformity on us all. People who have grown up in this country have gone to the same schools, watched the same television shows and movies, read the same magazines, shared the same historical events, taken in the same nightly news, worked for the same companies, been subjected to the same advertisements, celebrated the same holidays, and speak the same language.

Americanization

In many ways, the habits of Americans are a product of affluence and are spreading to other parts of the world. Extended families are less likely to live together when they can afford separate homes. It doesn't seem so bad to be alone when you're home with a radio, a television, and books and magazines you know how to read. Small families indulge their children more than large ones ever could, and children who own cars become less dependent on their parents.

In other countries, when jobs become available for young people in distant cities, when television begins to dominate home life, when ready-made foods appear in the markets, the culture appears more "American" – although the resemblances could be entirely superficial.

— Chapter Four —

HOW TO TELL AN AMERICAN

How is it that on any train platform in the world everyone can pick out the Americans? Despite all our different heritages, there is a style that marks us. We have shy people and bold, talkative and taciturn, and yet the quality of Americanness is unmistakable. The expression, the gestures, and the posture all give us away even before we speak.

The Famous Friendliness
One distinguishing characteristic of Americans is our openness to strangers. Practically everyone agrees that Americans are friendly.

Very few Americans care to put on snobbish airs, even if they secretly regard themselves as far above the crowd. Part of being superior is to appear not to think you are. The President of the USA emphasizes what a regular guy he is. A college professor who goes fishing with plumbers will brag about it; he too is one of the boys, not an intellectual in an ivory tower.

Thus the friendly "Hi" to whomsoever may cross our paths. It's a demonstration that we too subscribe to the creed of equality. It's an acknowledgement that whoever you are, you have rights. It does not mean that we owe you anything.

Foreigners find it striking that on city streets, people will nod and smile to them. Certainly if you pass someone on a lightly traveled way, you are expected to acknowledge him in some way.

Not to say hello to a neighbor is a breach of etiquette. On the street where I work, there is a building occupied by natives of a certain foreign country. These people have earned the enmity of the rest of the block simply by not greeting us. In their country, you don't greet people you don't know; here, they are considered unpleasant people, despite the fact that if someone were in need, they would probably be the first to help.

Friendly – Not Friends

Saying hello doesn't commit you to anything. It only asserts that you subscribe to our code of democracy. Friendliness should not be confused with friendship. Many foreigners slip up here, and mistakenly think that that boundless cordiality means they're going to have lots of friends. Then they become disillusioned and think we're terribly superficial and shallow in our friendships. But most of the people we refer to as "friends" are really acquaintances. True friends are not easier to come by here than anywhere else.

Emotions

Americans do not consider it necessary to hide their emotions. On the contrary, they often seem to be exaggerating them. Enthusiasm, for instance, rises to levels of seeming unbelievability ("It's *great* to see you. You look *fabulous*. Let's have lunch soon.")

For a girl in particular, it is desirable to have what is called a "bubbly" personality. The above glad sentiments don't mean much more than, "It is agreeable to be having this exchange on the street corner, and I may or may not be serious about lunch." The pleasantries are not phony as they leave both parties with a nice glow. Americans will even verbalize their warmth in statements such as "I like you" (which convinces the Asian that we're excessive for sure).

Happiness can be loudly proclaimed in big smiles, gestures, and statements: "This is marvellous, best news I've ever heard." Unlike many Asians, Americans smile only around good news or happy feelings. An American smiles often, but not when embarrassed or confused, nor would an American deliver bad news with a smile. Bad news comes with a somber, concerned expression.

My Indian friend – a longtime resident here – observed an Indian family reuniting at the airport. Although she knew they were overjoyed, she remarked on how subdued they were compared to American families who were whooping and hugging and talking all at the same time.

Expressing sadness does not come as easily to us. Sorrow interferes with our upbeat, optimistic view of life, and people who are sad do not find ready acceptance.

Touching

Americans are what is known as a "non-contact people." Outside of hugs given in greeting and parting, touching – among adults – is generally limited to occasions when its sexual connotations are acceptable. If in a moment of warmth, a Russian man rests his hand on an American man's thigh, the American is stricken. Could this be an untoward advance? Likewise, two American men would never hold hands. Nor would two American women, although they would not be as put off by the whole idea as men are.

Men slap each other on the back, or squeeze another's shoulder, but they avoid any touching that could appear to have sexual connotations.

Latin Americans find us cold in this regard; many Americans are envious of people who can reach out freely and affectionately, but our strong sense of the private space around each person inhibits us. In conversation, Americans usually stand at least an arm's length apart and are made uncomfortable by people who press closer (unless the relationship is an intimate one). We are careful not to breathe into people's faces.

Children and pets are caressed freely, although revelations about sexual abuse of children have caused inhibitions to enter even here.

Talking

Because it is important to be assertive, Americans speak fairly loudly, at least compared to Thais or Malaysians. Foreigners sometimes mistake the loudness for anger when an American is only trying to make himself understood.

Anger itself, within limits, is much more acceptable among Americans than among most Asians. If someone thinks he has been wronged, he may feel called upon to show his feelings. This is not to say that we admire people who are out of control – a temper tantrum is not a pretty sight – but a justifiably angry person will not be condemned whereas someone who "lets people walk all over him" could be. A reputation for "blowing your top" in business will not necessarily impede your upward progress.

Photo: Kristy MacDonald

The man on the left may appear angry, but the other two aren't upset by his behavior. They know he is just making a point.

Americans also have more tonal variety in their speech than most Asians. Their voices can swoop and soar, landing with heavy emphasis on particular words. Thus indignation, excitement, enthusiasm, and anger are all recognizable just from the tone of voice.

We are taught to look into people's eyes during conversation. Someone who instead looks around or down appears shifty to us, although in fact one doesn't stare continuously at the other person, but glances elsewhere every few seconds.

Etiquette

As a low-context culture, we don't have many set routines for particular situations. Elaborate protocol cannot survive in a free-floating society. Formality seems undemocratic to us, and Americans dislike the rituals of etiquette, inculcated in childhood, that distinguish between classes in other societies. Easy manners contribute to the fluidity of our society.

On the whole, the lack of formality makes integrating easier for the foreigner. You don't have to walk around in fear of offending people. However, the advantage of a high-context culture is that a learned protocol saves you having to improvise your behavior. Americans are often at a loss for words. An African Zulu, on hearing of a death in someone's family, can instantly deliver an elaborate and beautiful speech. We mumble we're sorry and change the subject.

"Informal," of course, does not mean "mannerless." We would not be any sort of culture if we did not have some agreement as to what constitutes nice behavior. But most of the time, Americans will be very forgiving of awkward manners. We do not have the religious prohibitions that make innocent foreign behavior so shocking in some countries. Nothing but the flag is sacred in our public life and even the right to desecrate it is protected. To insult somebody's religion takes a conscious effort.

Politeness

Visitors usually find Americans, for all their informality, very polite. This reputation seems to rest largely on the great number of "Pleases" and "Thank you's" we deliver, but also on the general recognition given to strangers. One should be considerate of waiters, garage attendants, and household help as well as of doctors and senators. Americans are shocked to see the peremptory manner in which servants are treated in other countries.

Of course, whether you consider Americans polite depends on where you come from. Some Japanese find Americans so rude that they think they are being discriminated against when Americans are only acting normally. Politeness also depends on where you are. New Yorkers have a far-reaching reputation for rudeness, although they can also be surprisingly helpful.

One might fairly say that Americans are often more polite in their public discourse than in private. It's when you get inside the home that you sometimes find civility collapses. In fact, a few of our young people have such awful manners that they are not able to behave themselves in public or in private.

The Sixties

Civilized behavior suffered a setback in the sixties when the philosophy of the times opposed any constriction on behavior, and youth aspired to overthrow anything that smacked of class divisions or insincerity. The ethic of "do your own thing" called for originality in all matters.

For a young person to leap to his feet, look the new arrival in the eye, shake his hand, and say, "How nice to meet you" might not express his true feelings. Thus he stayed in his seat (to stand indicates respect), eyes on the television, and grunted "Hiya" with an airy wave. This supposedly not only proved that he was a man of the people, it showed that he was too honest to show respect where it had not been earned.

47

Parents with the sixties' ethic actually instructed their offspring to act only in accord with their sincere feelings. Now that they see the result, many are chagrined. Far from shining in new ways, these young people seem deprived. Unable to produce pleasing behavior even when they want to, their company is not sought after.

So now with amazement we witness etiquette classes for adults, attended by persons whose social discomfort impels them to register. The dancing schools of long ago are reopening. A newspaper column, "Miss Manners," is widely syndicated. We probably will not see gentlemen go back to tipping their hats to the ladies or children leaping to their feet when their elders enter a room, but no longer are good manners scorned.

You may be assured that your own gracious manners will be found delightful.

Taboos

There are few taboos for newcomers to think about. Nobody has to worry about using the left hand, showing the soles of the feet, touching someone's head, or any of those prohibitions that seem so mysterious to Americans abroad. There are, however, a few habits widely abhorred:

1. Do not belch, that is, let gas upward out of the stomach while making an attention-catching noise. Farting is unmentionably rude, if not always preventable.
2. Do not spit. You may well see someone spit in the street, but you will know from the act that that person has no class. A gentleman does not spit, even in his own backyard.
3. Do not make noise chewing gum. This is lowly behavior, sometimes indulged in by the upper classes, but objectionable nonetheless. Chewing gum in itself is not charming.
4. Do not stare (gaze fixedly at someone you are not talking to).
5. Do cover your mouth when you cough, sneeze, or yawn.
6. Do not whistle at women.
7. Gentlemen should take off their hats indoors.

Photo: Kristy MacDonald

Sneezing, coughing, and yawning all require that the mouth be covered. The hand may be open or in a fist. It is nice to also say, "Excuse me."

The Casual Life

Informality pervades our culture. The forms of our language do not change when we address a superior, as they do in many languages. People dress casually as much as possible. We use slang in nearly all circumstances. We slouch in chairs, lean against walls, and put our feet on desks.

There are, however, boundaries. In church, you sit up straight. You do not use slang when before a judge. If your boss comes into your office and puts his feet up on your desk, you are flattered; he regards you as an equal. But you don't put your feet up on his desk; you would be presuming too much on the relationship. A lot of these distinctions are subtle, and foreigners can step on toes by trying to become American-casual before understanding the culture very well.

Our degrees of casualness do leave a lot of room for confusion. Teachers who are informal ("Call me Janet") and friendly and open with their students want to be liked; they do not wish to be treated as any other friend. Should their students respond by becoming too personal or forward with the teacher, they will discover a frosty barrier.

Boye de Mente in his insightful book, *Etiquette and Ethics in Japan*, depicts the Japanese as difficult to penetrate on the outside and very open on the inside. Americans, he says, are the opposite. The top layer is very open and anyone can penetrate it. It is the inner layers that are hard to crack. Some Americans remain forever impenetrable.

Relaxed? No

Most of my countrymen will be eager to assure you that they live in a very casual, relaxed manner. This may be far from true. They may keep their houses spotlessly clean, dine every night at the stroke of six, and never open their doors to strangers, but it is an article of faith that the good life is the relaxed one. Relaxing is a synonym for having a good time, as seen in the many advertisements which picture people lying around in the sun.

In point of fact, relaxing is precisely what Americans are not very good at. It just doesn't fit in with our belief in progress. Americans take the utilitarian philosophy seriously, which is that only useful activities are valuable, meaningful, and moral. Unproductive activity is therefore useless, meaningless, and immoral.

It's hard to take it easy when time represents opportunity. The conviction that you succeed or fail by your own efforts – rather than by the whims of fate – is one that adds a degree of tension to life.

And without family and community to fall back on, success of some sort becomes critical.

The whole concept of achievement, whether in career or hobby (e.g. gourmet cooking), makes passing the hours in idle conversation seem like a waste of time. As that sage Ben Franklin said, "Time lost is never found again." Too much sitting around, and the American gets nervous and wants to be up doing something. Even on vacation, Americans want to "improve each shining hour." Said an Indian married to an American, "We went to see the Grand Canyon and as soon as we got there my wife wanted to go rushing down to the bottom. These Americans never relax."

A Tanzanian living in the USA says, "I have my beeper on 24 hours a day. Even when I'm in bed with my wife, I have to respond within three minutes should it sound. How can I relax?"

A group of Italian journalists I know say that they all follow the same pattern in the States. At first they are terribly exhilarated by the pace of life. After six months, they are exhausted. How, they want to know, do Americans keep up this relentless activity?

"I never knew how important a weekend could be," says a Chinese resident here. "There is so much pressure at work, one deadline after another."

And it was an American who said, "If it's Tuesday, this must be Belgium," a reflection on the attempt to see fourteen European countries in fourteen days.

It's not just that we work hard. Our leisure activities are equally demanding. Besides the pursuit of health and fitness, any number of adult Americans are taking night classes, attending lectures, involving themselves in children's schools, leading scout troops, running church groups, birdwatching, and redecorating. Weekends are full of camping, sports, and home improvement. Then when we get "all stressed out," we take another course – in yoga, meditation, or stress management.

The person who never relaxes may turn to drugs for help – hence

Photo: Kristy MacDonald

Gardening is a popular way to make leisure time productive. Besides providing an excuse for being outdoors, the results are highly visible.

we may have some clue to the popularity in American life of alcohol, cocaine, marijuana, and the "boob tube" (television), which induces a drug-like lethargy and a dullness of mind almost as effectively as the real drugs.

The family hot tub is the latest antidote. Adopted from Japanese baths, it is a tub full of circulating hot water, in which four or five people can sit. The effectiveness of the hot water is such that nearly anyone can relax in one. (The question on most people's minds when invited to an evening in someone's hot tub is whether or not they will be expected to wear a bathing suit. You should bring your bathing suit and if your hosts wear suits, wear yours. If they instead are nude, you can take your choice. Naturally, you do not stare under any circumstances.)

The Well Planned Life

Being casual also has nothing to do with leaving matters to chance. The Latin American attitude of *"Que sera sera"* ("What will be will be") gets no credence here. We feel the prizes are awarded to the go-getters, the energetic, the forethinking. Many people plan their whole lives with care – career, children, retirement.

The little things are planned too, which is why foreigners can find it so irksome to make social engagements with Americans. Datebooks are full of rigid plans, and the plans for self-improvement often take precedence over the social ones.

Self-Improvement

It is doubtful whether there is anywhere else in the world a people so intent on improving themselves. Americans' nearly unique belief in progress includes the proposition that individuals can change their natures – or failing that, at least their bodies.

Foreigners tend to be skeptical of these American efforts. A Russian I interviewed said, "The kinds of self-improvement people go in for here are just superficial fads. My idea of self-improvement is moral."

It is true that not many people are intent on becoming better (i.e., more loving, self-sacrificing). Few of us want to live for others. Psychologists have made saintliness unfashionable by determining that it's the maladjusted person who wants to be a saint. They say that we must love ourselves before we can love other people. So we are trying to.

Foreigners usually think that Americans are quite good at loving themselves already, but they may mistake the outer bluster for the real thing. Actually, the competitive atmosphere in which we live makes people very critical of themselves. Depression is a major problem, particularly among women. Furthermore, the belief in progress suggests that life ought to be constantly getting better and better. As it usually isn't, we must find what's wrong and repair it.

53

It may be, as many foreigners claim, that Americans simply make problems for themselves. With plenty to eat and a good job, what could be wrong? But affluence brings problems of its own, for one the realization that money isn't everything. Many people never get this far, and continue to think that if they only had a little more money they'd be happy.

One must suspect that there is some grave difficulty in American culture that large numbers of people are searching with some desperation for self-fulfillment. It is likely that in the single-minded pursuit of achievement, important aspects of life are neglected.

Modes of Repair

Popular psychology has lined the bookshelves with volumes promising to bring happiness into individual lives. Most of them have to do with modes of right thinking. They teach how to be more assertive and to get the things out of life one deserves. Rather incredibly to the foreigners who feel that we're already the most selfish people in the world, many of these "philosophies" train people how to say no when other people make demands on them. A few popular favorites are: *How to Say No and Not Feel Guilty*, *Codependent No More*, and *Women Who Love Too Much*.

A perennial favorite for the past fifty years has been *How to Win Friends and Influence People* by Dale Carnegie. It's the basic textbook for popularity, and Dale Carnegie courses, which teach the techniques, are flourishing.

Weekend workshops cover all the same subjects that the books do, at much greater cost but promising a nearly instant new self. The past decade saw an emphasis on books and courses that straightforwardly promised to make a person rich (often presumed now to be the same thing as happy). There is instruction in time management, negotiation, sex (*The Joy of Sex*, a how-to by Alex Comfort was a bestseller in the seventies), and many words have been written on making relationships work.

Therapists

When troubles get too big, many Americans go off to see a therapist. There's a broad selection of them: doctors trained in psychoanalysis, psychologists, people with master's degrees in family therapy and social work. The range of methods used is likewise broad.

Foreigners are prone to think that Americans see therapists in situations when other peoples would talk to friends or family. The Americans, they assert, are too distant from family and too loath to burden their friends with their troubles.

It's true that many people would hesitate to impinge too much on a friendship, but the reason for seeing a therapist is also that the therapist is trained to bring a depth of understanding to the situation that the friend does not. Americans believe that once they have insight into their problems, they can change their self-destructive patterns.

There is no overwhelming evidence that therapy is terribly successful, but it obviously makes a lot of people feel better or they wouldn't continue to pay the high prices ($80 an hour is common) charged by therapists. For many people, it really is a last resort out of their miseries and may make life endurable until something else changes.

Exercise

Many people have concluded that exercise is even better than therapy. It doesn't seem surprising that after a few generations of riding around in cars and living in one-story houses, Americans would discover that they have lost a sense of physical wellbeing.

A few years ago, doctors delivered the news that the post-industrial age had produced physically well cared for but sadly unfit beings. Furthermore, they said, the American heart was in as bad shape as the rest of the muscles. The American male, it seemed, was inclined to drop dead before men in the rest of the westernized countries.

Photo: Kristy MacDonald

Joggers can be seen on city streets from early morning until late at night.

The answer, we were told, was aerobic exercise. (Aerobic exercise is the kind that raises the pulse to a certain level for a certain period of time, thus giving the heart itself a workout. It is also said to increase the brain's production of norepinephrines – natural tranquilizers.) Jogging was the first great craze. Then came stationary bicycles and rowing machines. Swimming has always been in style. The latest is aerobic dance, in which a roomful of sweating men and women run and kick and jump to loud, throbbing music.

Innumerable health clubs have opened in the last few years. Many use high-pressure tactics to sign newcomers up for an extended period. Some have initiation fees, large or small. Nearly all have some scheme whereby you can try out the club before joining.

Dieting

According to surveys, half the women in America believe themselves to be overweight. While we live in a country of great abundance, it is fashionable to be very thin. (Whatever you do, don't tell people they look fat.) The effort to be thinner than nature intended has put many people (usually women) on recurrent cycles of weight loss and regain. (While the woman may want to be thin, her under-nourished body clamors for food so the most common result of dieting is to make the dieter extraordinarily hungry.)

Despite evidence that at least 95% of the weight lost in dieting is regained, Americans remain irresistibly attracted to new diets and weight loss gimmicks. The top-selling kinds of books in this country are l) cookbooks and 2) diet books. There are indeed a large number of obese people in this country. People from many cultures get fat here, including ones that have little obesity back in their homelands.

There is an unfortunate prejudice against fat people, which comes from failure to understand that the fat person is a victim of a metabolic problem, not a person lacking in self-control. Foreigners in particular, surprised to see so much obesity, often suffer from this prejudice.

The Youth Cult

The elderly are also the victims of prejudice. The bias towards youth is so prevalent that even young men with a few grey hairs may dye their hair. At the very top, in the executive boardrooms, signs of age are permissible, but in most endeavors, older people – experience notwithstanding – are at a disadvantage.

Distressing as this is, it is not surprising in a country primarily interested in the new. Old people, who represent continuity with the past, have less to offer than in a culture where tradition is valued. Young people are not attached to the old ways of doing things, and their flexibility is considered an important asset.

We have enormous faith in new ideas, new techniques, and new gadgets. If schools aren't trying to solve their problems by imposing new teaching methods, they're trying to solve them by bringing in new computers. Advertisements will make their entire claim for a product the fact that it is NEW. They don't even have to add "Better." To us, "new" assumes "better." If nothing else, young people are newer, and even their unoriginal ideas may look new.

I have a friend, a very successful editor, who says that because she has reached the age of 40 without becoming an editor-in-chief, she can now reach the top only under the most extraordinary circumstances. Publishers are looking for 35-year-olds to run their shows. Discouraging as this seems, it is not true in every business.

Forever Young

The desperation to look young intensifies yearly. Facelifts, once the province of the very rich, are now undergone by ordinary middle-class people. A range of operations tackle other signs of aging.

Wrinkles are the great enemy, and for their elimination millions of dollars of dubious creams and potions are sold. Hair dye has made grey-haired women scarce.

Although most older women wouldn't wear knee socks and mini-skirts, they are not expected to adopt age-appropriate garb. No one would think that bright colors were more suitable for a young woman, or that the woman of years should not be wearing tight blue jeans and a blouse with a plunging neckline.

All people like to hear about how very young they look. One views old age as a stage of life when one is not in demand, when one has nothing to contribute. In a society where achievement is everything, those who are past contributing fall from grace.

Despite all this, there are many old people living enviably – active, busy, traveling, and contributing. There are others whose acquired wisdom is sufficient to sustain them and who remain admired by younger people. It is most noticeably those without health or money whose lives are the most pitiable.

— Chapter Five —

THE FAMILY

Nearly all Americans have a family somewhere, but it's often far from evident. The lack of strong family ties is one thing that strikes nearly all visitors to America (with the exception of those from Sweden, where apparently the family is even less demanding).

When an American speaks of "my family," he probably means his immediate, nuclear family: the group that lives together in one household – father, mother, and children. The larger family – the grandparents, aunts, uncles, and cousins – are often far away. Or even if nearby, they can be a small presence in each other's lives, visiting back and forth very little.

Photo: Marcia Lieberman

The ideal American family. Although these people may see other relatives on holidays, just the four of them feel self-sufficient as a family.

There are plenty of exceptions to this configuration: large families that have lived for generations in one town and gather together in all their spare moments. But in the large cities, each small family is more often floating free of the hometown connections. And to a much greater degree than in many countries, individual members of the family carry on a social life apart from the others.

If you make American friends, you may know them for a long time before meeting their families. Various members of the family with different interests expect to have different friends. Perhaps two couples socialize together, but instead the wives may lunch together or the husbands play golf, and the children never meet.

"Don't these Americans ever sit down and eat a meal with their families?" asks one Italian woman I know. Yes, many of us do, but according to the statistics, not regularly.

Nonetheless, the family remains the entity we fall back on. Holidays, weddings, and funerals bring the family together, and in times of trouble we turn to our families. But the trail of obligation generally runs only between parents and children. Few people feel much sense of duty to members of the extended family.

Marriage

The couple has to find each other, and it isn't always easy. Nearly all marriages are of two people who fall in love, but the great complaint of young – and middle-aged – people is that it is hard to meet other "singles." College is a golden opportunity, but after college there are fewer meeting points. Without a community life, it is perfectly possible for young working people to simply not meet other marriageable people. If their workplace doesn't produce candidates, their main hope is parties (not so good for shy people), pickup bars (not so good for respectable people), and coincidence (trains, parks, etc.)

This very real problem has produced entire sections of newspapers and magazines full of personal advertisements in which "Good-humored 36-year-old male seeks slender, sports-loving female, aged 25-35, who enjoys sunset walks, romantic dining, and movies. No smokers. Serious commitment wanted."

The Couple

Once joined, an American couple expect to be happily married, and to a large degree, they are. The obvious reason for this is the prevalence of divorce. If a couple gets along badly, they do not feel they must spend the rest of their lives together. This was not always so; to have "failed at marriage" was a social stigma thirty years ago, and for this and other reasons more of the unhappily married stayed married. Since then, the American divorce rate has tripled.

The American idea of a well-matched couple (Raymonde Carroll elaborates on this in her brilliant book, *Cultural Misunderstandings*) is one which always presents a united front to the world. Each member of the couple should be highly supportive of the other (in the same manner that "good" parents are supportive, rather than critical, of their children). They are expected to share a number of interests and activities and should spend vacations and weekend evenings together.

In public, the happy couple demonstrates coupleness with affectionate gestures and solicitude. At parties, they will often be found chatting in the same circle. The suspicion that they might not prefer each other's company to all others is cause for concern.

Because each American household operates so independently, the couple is thrown together an extraordinary amount. Indeed, they may have only each other to count on. The children grow up and leave home. Friends don't stop by. A Libyan I know, who lives in an expensive suburb, says she can't get over the fact that nobody ever comes to visit her neighbors. They rattle around by themselves in their large, elegant homes.

This isolation puts a lot of pressure on the married pair. If a couple is surrounded by a large family, their incompatibility is not so obvious as when they are constantly alone face to face. Of course, not every unhappy couple divorces. Many stay together out of a sense of duty, for financial or family reasons, or simply because they don't want to face life entirely alone.

A good many of those who do divorce never remarry. Thus one out of four American households with children is headed by a single adult. (In some of these, the parent never married.) Any foreigners thinking favorably of the American habit of divorce should note that some recent studies suggest that the children suffer long-term disadvantages. On average, they grow up much poorer than those in two-parent families, have less chance of going to college, and are less likely to have satisfactory marriages themselves.

Living Together

In the last twenty years, society has ceased to frown on sexual relations between unmarried adults, and many couples live together without getting married. A minority continue to live together indefinitely without marriage, but most of these arrangements conclude either at the altar (i.e., in marriage) or in dissolution. Most people still want their children to have properly married parents.

Blended Families

The "blended" family occurs when divorced parents marry, uniting their children into one household. Such families have many inherent problems. The step-parents are often resented and somewhere else the children have another parent, who is apt to be on bad terms with his/her former spouse. At best, the children adjust, but the complications of blended families are many.

Housework

The division of housework poses a problem in many American households. Before the Women's Liberation movement, women did nearly all of it while men were expected to take care of the outdoor work – despite the almost total lack of outdoor work in urban households. Now that so many women have jobs, most people agree that housework should be shared. However, old habits die hard. In actual fact, the women still do nearly all the housework and childcare, although in younger couples the men contribute more than their fathers did.

Babies

In the last twenty years, men have become involved in childbirth, and it is now normal for the father to be present in the delivery room, which has become a more humane place than it used to be. Most people aspire to natural childbirth (that is, with as few drugs as possible), although births still usually take place in hospitals, in

Photo: Marcia Lieberman

"Good" husbands accompany their wives to childbirth classes and are present while the baby is born. They may learn breathing exercises that help their wives relax during delivery.

case of complications. Some parents now choose to have midwives, rather than doctors, preside over the delivery.

If all goes well, women leave the hospital very shortly after giving birth. At least half of them breastfeed their babies, another revolt against modern, commercial methods. There is no prohibition against women leaving the house in the weeks after childbirth, and they may return quickly to active lives.

Professional couples often put off having children until they are in their thirties or even forties and then generally feel that one or two children are enough. The long-awaited baby is much doted on and causes a drastic change in its parents' lives. The new parents who formerly went out to dinner nearly every night and saw every new movie stay home and talk baby talk.

Daycare

Just over half of American mothers with children under five years old have jobs, a dramatic increase in the last thirty years. Many go back to work in the first few months of their new babies' lives. As only a quarter of these have mothers, husbands, or other relatives able and willing to look after the baby during the day, finding good childcare has become a giant problem.

The government operates very few daycare centers, and these are reserved for low-income families. A miniscule number of workplaces provide daycare facilities. There are numerous private daycare centers, but the staff is often underpaid and weary from looking after too many children. Few of these accept infants or toddlers who aren't toilet trained. Cooperative daycare centers have the advantage of high parent supervision, but parents must be able to contribute a certain amount of time each week.

Parents who can afford to will try to hire someone to come into their home and look after baby, but good caretakers are hard to find and keep. Sometimes two sets of parents will share one caretaker. Alternatively, the parents may take their child to the home of someone who takes in one or more children during the day.

In recent years, there has been much reporting of sexual and physical abuse in daycare centers. How much of this reporting is accurate and how much abuse really takes place is unknown. At any rate, parents should be extremely careful in selecting a daycare center. The chances that your child will suffer overt abuse are low, but it is quite possible that your child will receive less loving attention than you would wish. You should be very suspicious of any center that does not welcome unexpected parental visits or tries to keep the parents at an arm's length from the classrooms.

Photo: Marcia Lieberman

Children too young for school whose parents work often spend their days in "daycare centers" where they are cared for by paid workers.

Babysitters

The whole concept of evening babysitters is a novelty to many foreigners, to whom the thought of leaving children with a stranger is horrible. What would be horrible to us is never getting away from the kids. Lacking a supply of relatives to look after them, we hire somebody, which has the further benefit of allowing us to pay and not build up any obligations.

The person might be the older child of neighbors, a babysitter recommended by friends, or a student from a nearby college. If the first time goes well, we try to hire the same babysitter again so he or she doesn't remain a stranger long. But as long as the person is reliably recommended, we don't worry overly about the stranger aspect. American children are supposed to learn to relate to many different people.

The usual routine with a babysitter is to leave a phone number where you can be reached in an emergency, instructions for children's bedtimes, etc., and an invitation to "help yourself to anything in the refrigerator." You should have established when you first spoke how much you pay per hour (you'll have to find out what local terms usually are). You are responsible for seeing that the babysitter gets home safely – meaning either you drive him/her or provide taxi fare.

Bringing Up Children

Foreigners are shocked when they first arrive and hear children say things to their parents like, "Boy, Dad, you're really dumb," or "Are we going to have that crud for dinner?" (In fact, many Americans also are taken aback by such talk.) One of the most dubious propositions of the sixties was that children were among the downtrodden groups. "Children's rights" became an issue, and there are still some parents who feel that their young children should enjoy unlimited free speech and choice.

But even apart from this peculiarly democratic outlook, the

upbringing of an American child is quite different from that of a Thai, Chinese, French, or Brazilian child. In most of the countries of the world, parents feel that their obligation is to raise an obedient child who will fit into society. The little ego must be molded into that of a well-behaved citizen.

Not so here. Although there are many things a child must learn – from eating with a knife and fork to driving a car – the top priority is to raise an individual capable of taking advantage of opportunity. Such a person cannot be overly obedient or hindered by too-great family attachments. American life is marked by change and those who thrive are self-sufficient, quick jumpers, who can exist – if need be – far from family. Children are taught to be autonomous rather than to fit into the group.

Self-Discovery

Parents feel an obligation to give their children every opportunity to blossom. Blossoming takes time and a lot of scope. Parents do not feel that they can dictate a child's path; our belief in individuality requires that each person figure out his own direction. We regard abilities as widely varying – one person may be cut out to be a law professor, another could be a genius as a car mechanic. (This is contrary, for instance, to the Japanese who think that almost anyone who makes an effort can do almost anything.)

The child must get the chance to find his niche. This means leaving him or her free to experiment, to try one thing and then another. We (at least in theory) resist the kind of tracking that in many countries directs children along career paths at young ages. If you're going to fulfill your potential – the object in life here – you can't settle down too early.

We also consider it important not to break a child's spirit. A child who is too demure and obedient will not have the audacity to go far in this society. It takes self-confidence to start your own company, to think of new ways to split atoms, to play in a rock band.

So parents try to emphasize the positive. Rather than pointing out to a three-year-old that his picture of a house ought to have a roof, we declare it the most magnificent picture of a house ever and tape it to the refrigerator. We want each child to feel that he is a very special child, with unique, notable abilities. After all, self-promotion goes a long way, even in lieu of talent.

The independence starts young. Rather than being held all day long, babies are put in strollers or baby carriers. At night, they sleep in their own cribs, ideally in their own rooms. Theoretically, babies who are left to cry rather than being picked up will learn to console themselves: the first lesson in self-reliance. As soon as children begin to speak, they are encouraged to express their own opinions and desires. Each child has his own toys, which he is not forced to share if he doesn't want to, although parents will be disappointed by evidence of selfishness.

Privacy and private property are both considered sacrosanct. A child may refuse to allow anyone into his room. It is considered poor behavior on the part of a parent to read a child's diary or mail without permission. Parents shouldn't be too nosy. It is taken for granted that children will have secrets from their parents.

Many parents do not believe in spanking and will carry on long dialogues with the child about misbehavior in situations when many foreigners would report, "I smacked him once and he never did it again." Taking advantage of physical superiority doesn't seem right to Americans, who also have deep fears of becoming child abusers.

The freedom of choice given American children is striking – and often shocking – to foreigners. Some parents do seem to carry it to such extremes that their regard for their children's safety appears warped, but the hope is to develop maturity through experience. Learning through failure is the American way. Abraham Lincoln failed at many enterprises before becoming President. "Nothing ventured, nothing gained" is an old saying.

Who's In Charge Here?

Often one sees an American engaged in a dialogue with a tiny child. "Do you want to go home now?" says the parent.

"No," says an obviously tired, crying child. And so parent and child continue to sit discontentedly in a chilly park.

"What is the matter with these people?" says the foreigner to himself, who can see the child is too young to make such decisions. Although one indeed wonders, the child is acquiring both a sense of responsibility for himself and a sense of his own importance. Sensible parents modulate decision making according to age, but the attitude that "it's up to you" is much more prevalent than elsewhere.

In the end, the child must be responsible for his own life, and his parents worry if he remains dependent on them in any way. They will not take credit for his successes (although they probably will feel guilty if he fails) nor will they feel that he should be particularly grateful for their contribution.

Photo: Marcia Lieberman

Parents try to give serious attention to their children's thoughts and feelings.

The Spoiled Child

Ideally, the American system produces self-confident, capable people. However, it doesn't always, and foreign visitors frequently remark that American children are spoiled. It is true that demanding, tyrannical children are not uncommon.

American parents do not have the confidence they once had regarding child raising. During this century, child psychologists, educators and doctors have become the experts on bringing up children.

The experts taught that the child's emotional stability should be the chief goal; children not listened to and understood would be psychologically damaged. Above all, the child had to be convinced that his parents would love him no matter what he did (this was to instill basic self-confidence). The pressure to please Mommy and Daddy considerably lessened.

At the same time, parental ties to community and larger family (and frequently to each other) were breaking down, and so the parents themselves were becoming less secure. They were increasingly unwilling to be authorities, sometimes unpopular ones, in their children's lives. They wanted their children to be their friends. They did not like to say "no."

Furthermore, time to spend with the children shortened. In many families, both parents have jobs, and the average workday has grown longer. Only rarely are there other relatives to fill in the gap, and many children spend long hours in daycare or come home after school to an empty house. On weekends, there is less time for family outings than in the old days.

Appliances and urban living have freed children from chores so schoolwork is their main obligation (and by most standards, there's not much of that). Most parents are loath to impose any hardship on their children. Toys are cheap so in this age of abundance – and smaller families – children have emerged with roomfuls of stuff, including stereos and personal televisions. If one is inclined to spoil

71

the children, it is very easy to do so, unlike in a society in which the child's labor is needed and toys are few.

The Re-Invention of Discipline

On the positive side, many people of all ages have good relationships with their parents, far friendlier than in cultures in which the parents, often fathers in particular, are remote authorities. But where "spoiling" rather than understanding is the norm, some unpleasant children have emerged: undisciplined, self-centered, and unhappy. Recently, the experts have turned around and discovered "limits," concluding that children are happier when they have parents who act like parents and give them rules and structure.

Newcomers to the United States should take heart that more Americans are rejecting total indulgence. If you are "strict," you may be in the minority, but you are not alone. Do not let your children persuade you that all American parents let their children do anything they want.

Television

Many social analysts now think that the television's domination of the American home is at the root of many of the country's problems. Television rivals family and church as the dispenser of values. Repeated thousands of times a day in advertisements is the message that acquiring stuff is a worthy social goal. It is a message that children are very susceptible to, and the longing of even young children for certain brand names is a product of television.

Situation comedies depict children as fearless loudmouths who outsmart their parents. The television children live in large, beautiful homes and wear snazzy clothes. They don't clean the bathroom and spend little time on their homework. What child would prefer his own family to the idealized television family?

The family meanwhile is listening to the television voices instead of talking to each other. As Marie Winn, author of *The Plug-In*

Drug, says, "Family life becomes parallel rather than interactive."

Children who watch television are found to have much poorer imaginations than those who don't. Teachers report as well that television watchers have short attention spans. Just as television must amuse every second, now the teacher must be fast-paced and entertaining.

Actual neurological damage can result from spending the formative years in front of the television. In the absence of playtime and dialogue, the child does not develop normally, and the amount of violence on television gives viewers a distorted outlook on the world.

If children spend hours per day in the most effortless manner possible – watching television – they cannot be expected to be very good at making a rigorous effort on demand. Thus American children, who can be very bright and intuitive, are often not inclined to apply themselves to the hard stuff – such as learning their multiplication tables or studying spelling words. Or even reading books. This gives a great advantage to immigrant children who are capable of hard work and capture a remarkable number of the academic prizes. Two of the winners of a recent national spelling contest were from Vietnam.

I once asked a roomful of immigrants in an English class, who all objected to the low quality of American television, why they did not just get rid of the household television. They laughingly admitted that the whole family had become addicted to it. Foreigners some-times feel that its value as an English teacher overrides its disadvan-tages, but that seems optimistic, considering the number of people who have the television on all day and still don't speak English.

Concerned American parents severely restrict their children's television watching. Studies regularly show that the children who watch the least television have the greatest academic and personal success. A small elite in the country have banished television from their homes altogether.

Teenagers

The teenage years are apt to be difficult for Americans. Delightful as it may seem to be on the threshold of total independence, in fact it can be frightening. Teenagers are aware that they have the task of fulfilling some large potential, but there is nobody to tell them what it is. Many will be going on to college, but they feel pressure to make a mark at a young age. It is a much more serious time of life for Americans than for some other nationalities, who see it as a last chance for good times before settling down.

The American teenager, who is expected ultimately to separate psychologically from his family, withdraws a great deal from them during the teen years. For his own self-respect he must resist family activities. Many teenagers are splendidly responsible and mature, but simply being a teenager is an excuse for anti-social behavior. "It's his hormones," say the parents. Many parents give up trying to influence their teenage children.

One theory for the distress among American teenagers is that, while they are no longer children, they have no real function or responsibility in society. Time hangs heavily on their hands while they wait for adulthood.

It's the peer group that becomes all-important. Both boys and girls spend hours in front of the mirror and adhere to rigid standards of dress that identify them with certain groups. They would spend all their time with their friends if they could. Popularity is terribly important. They identify themselves with their chosen group through music, clothes, slang, and activities – nearly all selected from a world totally alien to the adult world.

Not all teenagers, however, are solely absorbed in teen life. There are a heartening number who give time to good causes, evidence concern for the larger world, and are ethical, imaginative, and hardworking. Many teenagers have alert social consciences and are quick to challenge injustice.

Photo: Esther Wanning

Teenagers are paid by their parents to do chores. The money they earn goes mostly towards entertainment, such as musical tapes and tickets to movies.

Teenagers often have jobs, not because their families are unable to support them, but in order to have spending money. Parents are generally happy to have their children work; it's another sign that the kids are becoming independent, it gives them responsibility, and it keeps them out of trouble. Teenagers are usually paid by their parents for mowing the lawn, washing the car, and often for babysitting for younger siblings.

Older teenagers, even those from wealthy families, want to have summer jobs. The well-connected ones, however, will teach swimming at their family's country club or work in their father's law office rather than work at McDonald's. The teenager who is not working in the summer will be expected to carry on some other worthwhile activity – such as travel or study.

Sex

Although "dating" seems less in vogue than it once did, with young people hanging around in groups instead, some teenagers begin to date as early as 13 or 14 years of age. Most parents, however, do not encourage their children to have dates until they are in high school. The extent of the date depends on age and parental permissiveness, but most parents see no harm in their youngsters pairing off at a young age – as long as the affair does not become too serious. Most children have a curfew by which they are to be home.

A side effect of the sexual revolution was that teenagers began to feel that it was their right – if not their duty – to be having sex. Whereas thirty years ago it was considered a moral failing to engage in intercourse before marriage, now even many teenage girls would prefer not to be virgins. One result is that teenagers give birth to nearly a half million babies annually.

However, foreigners should not assume that a date equals sex here in America. The more sensible teenagers are quite capable of restraining themselves and see the virtue in doing so – or at least use condoms and are very discriminating about their partner. And the presence of AIDS and other diseases has given further weight to the arguments against teenage sex. What is more, teenagers continue to be as nervous as they ever were around the opposite sex.

Drugs

The other great threat on parents' minds is drugs. A variety of illegal drugs are widely available, and many teenagers use them. Whether or not drugs are considered "cool" varies in different schools and communities. Besides alcohol, the most widely used drug is marijuana. The usual effect of marijuana is to make the user inarticulate and passive. You can sometimes tell by the redness of the eyes if someone is "high."

In the last few years, crack – a cheap and extremely addictive form of cocaine – has seized hold in the poorest areas and caused incredible damage to young lives and their communities. As yet, it is not prevalent in the suburbs.

There are many more teenagers who have tried drugs than who continue to use them. There are a few who become quickly addicted, steal to support their habits, and drop out of school – but these were not generally happy and well-adjusted children in the first place. If your children are doing well and have a loving family, it is highly unlikely that they are going to become drug addicts just because the opportunity presents itself.

The Foreigners' Despair

To great numbers of immigrants to America, the worst part of life here is seeing their children bring home American attitudes of disrespect towards their parents. When the Korean father says to his son, "Come home right after school," and the son replies, "You can't make me," it is extremely disheartening, particularly as society does not seem to be on the father's side.

In Korea, the son would never have defied his father. Here, immigrant children soon get a taste of the freedom American children enjoy and want the same. Whether or not they insist on it, the different standards nearly all cause family conflict. "We want to have fun, but our parents just want us to stay home," a Cambodian lamented.

It is inevitable that the children will want to be more like Americans than their parents are. The teenage world here is a demanding one, and the new immigrants are trying to fit in. At the same time, children who are taught to respect their own culture will probably appreciate the closeness of their families and ultimately, perhaps after a painful period, work out their differences.

It is better if the parents are not too rigidly attached to the way things were done back home. At the same time, they should not feel they need to drop their standards altogether. Children who can combine American opportunities with their own family support structure will be well poised for success in America.

The Young Adult

In the 19th century, there were very few fields that required a college degree. A heavy dose of professionalism has now crept into our society, and even people applying for middle manager positions are asked to have a college diploma. An advanced degree is required to demonstrate expertise at anything at all. Consequently, parents gear themselves up to make great sacrifices to see that their children are college-educated.

Many young people contribute to their expenses while in college by working. There is no disgrace in holding down some menial job while "getting an education." As a matter of fact, it is a badge of honor to have worked one's way through college.

Moving Out

For economy, young people may live at home during college years, but for many the college is a long way from home. Those who have finished their schooling may find apartments of their own, often shared with other young people. The fact that their new housing may be far less luxurious than their parents' home is unimportant compared to gaining adult status.

Their careers – or the appeal of a more glittering city – may cause many to move to another city or state, the start of an odyssey that may keep them forevermore at a distance from the family, although they will visit on holidays. Once they have left home and are self-supporting, parents no longer feel responsible for them.

Parents are unlikely to make major sacrifices for their children after providing an education. Our confidence in the American way is such that we believe the deserving can and will succeed, without family interference. And because success is defined by achievement, not by family status, parents fear to inhibit the young person's efforts by "handing it to them on a silver platter."

Just the Cash, Please

Many parents do help their grown children with small outlays of cash. Some foreigners find it strange that the tables don't turn at a certain point so that the young people are helping their parents. One reason is that, on average, today's young adults are poorer than their parents, who years ago were able to buy houses cheaply at low interest rates. At the same time, the younger people have higher expectations than their parents did and feel entitled to more cars, bathrooms, restaurant dinners, and vacations to faraway places than anyone used to.

Whatever their relative financial positions, few adult children welcome unsolicited advice from their parents. They were raised to make their own decisions and most do. Some parents and children may discuss all subjects together, but the kind of relationship known in Asia in which the young defer to the old is rare. In fact, parents and adult children with poor relationships and little communication are not uncommon.

Grown children who remain residents of the parental home cause concern that they haven't acquired the self-reliance expected of them. There is a large new crop of these, causing a flurry of newspaper features. In the American mind, something has gone wrong when children prefer hanging around their parents and eating their mothers' cooking to going out and making an independent life for themselves. But since rents are high, and few parents regulate their grown children's sex lives, there's good reason to stay under the parental roof.

Any Roof but the Kids'

Old people tend to spend their days among other old people – or alone. The isolation of the old is astounding to many newcomers here. Traditional cultures would never think up such a thing as an old-age home, an establishment made up entirely of unrelated old people and their caretakers.

79

Photo: Marcia Lieberman

Old people hope to enjoy their leisure years and many move to the warmer southern climates.

However, you should not assume that old people are rejected because they're isolated. Whether or not the relationship is a happy one, grown children feel responsible for the care of aging parents (or at least for seeing that they get care). But independence is valued as much by the old as it is by the young. "I never want to be a burden on my children," is a common phrase on the lips of parents. To have to give up one's own home and go live with a son or daughter, subjected to the moods of badly behaved grandchildren, helpless against loud stereos, ever conscious that one is not a contributing member of the household – such is an unwanted fate.

Better to keep on in your own home, with all the effort and expense that entails. "Alone" may mean "lonely," but being lonely is better than loss of freedom. Many old people do have nearby relatives who help out, but the critical point is to remain in one's own home.

Even an old-age home is not always considered such a bad lot. Some are awful, but others are gracious and elegant – and expensive. Paying guests know that they are at least of financial worth to the institution, which is better than being a family dependant.

The children may even be financing their parents' stay in the institution, but by not having them under their own roof they are graciously according them some remaining autonomy. Just as their parents encouraged them to be independent at a young age, the children are now allowing the parents to be independent. Having finished with child raising, it is felt that the parents deserve to be around their own peer group – other old people – rather than to be bothered by young children.

There are a growing number of "retirement communities" which provide apartments in complexes designed just for old people. Many of these are in the balmier climates of the USA. No children are allowed (except as visitors), a rule set to please the old folks, who obviously do not delight in the pitter-patter of young feet as much as sentimentalists would like to think.

It's the poor (and recent immigrants who haven't acquired American ideas) who are most apt to spend their last years living with family members. The other options appear to be preferable to anyone who can afford them.

There is much talk these days about "the problem of old people in America." Part of the problem is that there are so many of them and in twenty years there will be many more. Because people are living to be so much older, many 60-year-olds with heart diseases of their own are concerned about parents in their eighties. Modern medicine has become very skilled at keeping very old people alive, but does not necessarily succeed at making them healthy. The result is that a large proportion of the country's medical care goes to people in their last years of life. Americans are peculiarly resistant to dying, and most die in hospitals while trying to prolong life at all cost.

Pets

It sometimes seems that the most popular member of the family is a dog. Considering how loyal, polite, and affectionate dogs are, this is not surprising. (Americans find the thought of eating dogs repugnant.) Cats are also full-fledged members of many families. When the pet dies, the family is genuinely grief-stricken.

Friends as Family

There are numerous people who claim, "My friends are my family." These people very likely have, somewhere, a real family, but they

Photo: Kristy MacDonald

Dogs are important members of many households.

feel much closer to their friends. American life changes greatly between generations. Parents who live in a Boston suburb, attend the Congregational Church, and have steak cookouts may not know what to make of a vegetarian daughter living on the West Coast who periodically visits her guru in India.

Less drastic differences than this cause alienation in families. Distance alone may account for loss of contact. Instead of family, groups of friends may get together for Thanksgivings and Christmases, go on trips together, and share joys and sorrows. This is particularly true for those who are single, whether before or after being married.

Despite the appeal of replacing an inconvenient family with carefully selected friends, there is a drawback: Friends cannot be expected to proffer as much aid as family. Those who claim to rely on their friends usually are highly independent, with good health and sound finances. Even the best of friends are keeping track of favors. Your sorrows are not their sorrows. In catastrophe, you are on your own and will probably turn to your real family. No matter how distant the family in America has become, it has not been replaced.

Chapter Six

DAILY LIFE

FOOD

American cuisine in itself is not bad. Our cooks have an abundance of fresh ingredients and a heritage of marvelous regional dishes: apple pie, clam chowder, Louisiana gumbo, barbecued oysters, corn fritters, strawberry shortcake, and countless other delectable dishes. As many guidebooks lamely say, it is possible to eat very well in America.

It is also possible to eat very badly, and many Americans do – by choice rather than necessity. A lot of supermarket food, while cheap and plentiful, is produced to provide the most calories with the longest shelf life and the shortest preparation time. The result is frozen dinners, packaged sweets, instant puddings, bottled salad dressings, and canned sauces. Manufacturers are working night and day to invent new products that will captivate the public. Almost any conceivable meal is available ready-made.

The problem is that none of this stuff is very good. It supplies calories, but in real satisfaction it doesn't measure up to anything fresh or homecooked. Even fruits and vegetables are raised to survive long shipping or storage periods, rather than for taste. Meats are tender and good (unless you like a gamey taste), but very fatty and distressingly laden with hormones and antibiotics. Also, most supermarket food is wrapped, canned, frozen, jarred, or packaged in such a way that you can't examine it until you get it home. (Many are so well sealed that they're maddeningly difficult to open even at home.) If you do try to open jars or poke into packages, management will be distressed.

If you come from the USSR, or another country with severe food shortages, you won't complain, but most foreigners find American food takes some getting used to.

Sweet and Bland

A Tanzanian said he found American food so bland he nearly starved when he first came. "Back then, I couldn't even find a bottle of Tabasco [a hot sauce] in my little town." Then he discovered pizza and survived. The American palate has become braver than it used to be, but in the average household you won't find much seasoning in use beyond salt and pepper.

And sugar. There seems to be no end to the march on sweetness. One food writer swears that at a banquet he attended he was served a cup of M&M's (little candies) for an appetizer. Americans are stuck on sugar, and sugar (or other sweetener) is added to most packaged foods. It's hard to find a snack that isn't sweet, and a number of main-course dishes are served with a sweetener – such as pancakes with maple syrup and lamb with mint jelly. American pastries are very sweet, and Americans eat sweet desserts much more regularly than most peoples.

A lot of sodium (an element in salt) is regularly added to packaged foods, which has caused such an outcry among doctors (too much is said to be bad for the heart) that new lines of foods are coming out advertising themselves as "sodium-free." There are also a lot of sugar-free foods, but you have to read labels carefully to make sure you aren't just getting honey or corn syrup or an awful-tasting artificial sweetener.

A law requires the contents of foodstuffs to be listed on the package, in the order of the greatest to the least quantity. It's enlightening reading.

Eating Habits

The first two meals of the day eaten by an American are generally quick. The classic American breakfast of bacon and eggs is seen more on weekends than when the whole family is rushing to school and work. Cereal with milk and a cup of coffee is probably the usual morning sustenance of the average American. Lunch consists of a sandwich, soup or salad. Dinner is the large meal of the day. (When the lunchtime meal is the big one it can also be called "dinner" and when the evening meal is simple it may be called "supper.")

The American dinner has fallen under medical disapproval due to its high cholesterol content. The meal typically consists of a large piece of meat, ketchup, vegetables with butter, potatoes (fried or with butter), and a sweet dessert. It might also be an equally fatty frozen meal, heated in the microwave oven, or a high-calorie pizza.

A large proportion of Americans report that they would like to change their diets, but habits are hard to break. The beans, vegetables, and whole grains that doctors keep urging us to eat require time to cook, which we haven't got. Take-out Chinese food may be as close as many Americans get to low-calorie, low-cholesterol meals.

Street Food

Many foreigners comment on how often Americans are eating as they walk down the street. If hungry, we grab something. There is always something to grab – from a hot dog stand, a doughnut shop, a corner store. The thing is rarely nutritious, but it stills the appetite for an hour or two. There appear to be people who rarely eat a whole meal at once. At home, they snack while standing in front of the open door of the refrigerator.

What seems to distress our foreign visitors about snacking is the lack of seriousness about food. For people who invest a great deal of time thinking about mouthwatering dishes shared with friends and family, the life of a snacker hardly seems worth living. To us, it's a life rich in efficiency, pared down to the essential elements. If only we could speed up sleeping.

Good Eating

There is, thankfully, another side to this story. Dismayed by a landscape of tasteless fast foods, a reaction has sprung up. It began with the appearance of health food stores, which stock foods in as close to their natural states as possible – whole-wheat flour and breads, organic produce (fruits and vegetables grown without chemical fertilizers or pesticides), and wide assortments of nuts, beans, and grains. A fringe group of eaters known as "health food nuts" only shop at health food stores.

The health food trend has come to supermarkets, and now some large chains carry eggs from uncaged chickens, peanut butter without additives, organic vegetables, etc. Once the customers materialized, specialty farms started to produce lovingly grown, tasty vegetables and even "organic" cattle and pigs.

Recent Asian and Middle Eastern immigrants have improved the quality of produce markets, and gourmet food stores and fresh fish markets have proliferated. Major cities have grocery stores selling staples for every kind of cuisine. It is possible to find excellent ingredients in most parts of the country – although it may take extra effort and money.

Foodies

There have recently sprung up among us a category of persons known as "foodies." Foodies are exacting about everything that passes their lips. They are on a voyage of discovery, constantly on the lookout for new and exotic foods: radicchio, sun-dried tomatoes, varieties of mushrooms. Cheeses alone absorb vast quantities of their attention. They eat only baby lettuce and fresh pasta. They watch famous chefs on television, cook, and explore new restaurants.

Because of the time and financial investment required of foodies, most are Yuppies (Young Upwardly Mobile Professionals) or Dinks (Double Income No Kids). Foodies are exceptions to all the rules about American eating, but only time will tell whether their interest lasts. The Yuppie attention span is notoriously fleeting.

Dining Out

Restaurant dining is not the natural heritage of the American, and constant eating out strikes us as somewhat lazy and thriftless. Nonetheless, as kitchen time disappears, restaurants are increasingly where Americans eat. In large cities you can partake of nearly any cuisine in the world; a small town may have a single diner.

The following categories start with the cheap and end with the high-priced.

Fast Food

Fast food establishments, such as McDonald's, Burger King, Wendy's, H. Salt Esq., Kentucky Fried Chicken, Pizza Hut, and Taco Bell purvey their specialties from coast to coast. Few urban areas are so small as not to be ringed with a few of them.

Each item, which you step up to a counter to order, is mass-produced according to an exact prescription. The menu, often illustrated, is permanently displayed above the counter. No alcohol is served. Your food comes with an almost equal weight of plastic and paper serving containers and cutlery, which you are expected to throw into the trash when you're finished. You should specify if you want your order to take out.

Fast food restaurants appeal greatly to juvenile tastes. The notorious plastic taste of much of the food offends gourmets, but these places do have the advantage of being clean and extremely cheap. No tipping is expected.

Coffee Shops

"Coffee shop" may be in the name, and it may not. A coffee shop is easily identifiable, however, by its seating arrangements (a counter, booths, and possibly some tables) and bright lighting. You needn't wait to be seated. In the classic coffee shop grey-haired waitresses call everyone "Honey," and cases of pies are lined up behind the counter. Sandwiches are the mainstay of the menu, although a short-order cook stands over the grill and turns out eggs, pancakes, burgers, and fries. Occasionally a coffee shop will have a dinner menu, but most aren't even open for dinner. The breakfasts are usually an excellent bargain. (Americans like going out to breakfast, especially on weekends.)

A waitress will often offer coffee as soon as you sit down. In the hospitable western part of the country, waitresses refill your coffee cup as fast as you can empty it. On the East Coast (where "regular" means with cream), you will have to pay for your second and third cups of coffee. However, you may find that one cup is more than enough as coffee shop coffee is not highly rated. (There are more and more cafés serving espresso opening up, but these usually feature expensive pastries and delicacies rather than hearty food.)

You may be able to order beer or wine in a coffee shop, but rarely hard liquor. Often you pay a cashier on the way out. You should leave a tip of about 15% on the table because it won't be included on the bill.

Photo: Esther Wanning

Distinctive little eateries such as this may be well worth stopping at. You are likely to find real people and real food. This particular one, in the state of Maine, features seafood and blueberry dishes.

Diners

Diners are the rural version of the coffee shop. They do their best to look like railroad passenger cars, and you should not shun one merely because it looks a little run-down on the outside. The food may be excellent, unlike at the fast-food franchise which always looks newly minted. Legend has it that you tell a good diner by the number of big trucks parked in front – truckdrivers are supposed to know where they'll get their money's worth, although it may be instead that their choice is based on the size of the parking lot. Still, a truck stop may be colorful and probably will be cheap.

Family Restaurants

This is an amorphous category, so-called because you can bring the kiddies, usually meaning a) the place is fairly casual; b) the bar, if any, is out of sight; c) a high chair is available for the baby; and d) the food is of the familiar American kind – chops, steaks, fried fish, salads, and potatoes. (The "family," however, does not include your dog, who is barred from all restaurants by sanitary codes.) Many family restaurants are Italian, and pizza and spaghetti now seem as American as apple pie.

On entering, you should wait to be seated. No matter how crowded the restaurant is, you won't be asked to share a table with another party, even if you're alone. If you spy a table you prefer to the one you're led to, feel free to speak up.

You'll probably get a basket of bread and a glass of water without asking. Menus are frequently large and elaborate, describing the food in superlatives ("cooked-to-perfection chicken breasts in mouthwatering cream sauce with garden-fresh vegetables"), but you should ignore the adjectives and try to figure out what the dish is.

You may have a choice of ordering a dinner or *à la carte*. If you order *à la carte*, you will be paying separately for the various components of your meal, such as the salad and dessert. The dinner, which costs more, includes the extra courses. Read the small print to find out what comes with what.

At this level of dining you may run into one of the new chummy waiters. Such a one will appear at your table and say, "Hello. How are you tonight? My name is Steve. I'm going to be your waiter. I'd like to tell you about our specials." (If he doesn't tell you the price of the specials, be sure to ask.) After his speech is over, he will behave much more like a real waiter – disappearing when you want him most – than a friend. You are not expected to introduce yourselves to him.

Your soup or salad will be served before the main course. Presumably this is to keep you happy while you're waiting. The drawback is that after bread and salad one is often too full to eat the rest of the meal. As large servings are a feature of family-style restaurants, you may want to ask for a "doggie bag" to take your leftovers home in. The waiter will whisk your plate away and bring back your dinner wrapped up – your next day's lunch.

Family restaurants have a pleasant lack of pretension and reasonable prices, but do not attract gourmet eaters. A 15% tip is sufficient, as in most restaurants.

The Ethnic Restaurants

In the big cities, you have your choice, from Afghan to Zimbabwean, with prices big and little. The Asian selection has particularly exploded in recent years, and in many of these a little money goes a long way. In the Southwest and California, there are also many wonderful Mexican and other south-of-the-border restaurants. In Middle America, Chinese may be your only choice when the urge for something foreign comes over you.

Regional Restaurants

Keep your eye out for regional specialties when you're traveling around the country. In the South you can hope to find hominy grits, black-eyed peas, mustard greens, southern fried chicken, sweet potato pie, okra soup, and numerous other specialties. (The South has some wonderful cafeterias you might want to try; most cafeterias in the North are of low quality.)

New England is known for corn, clam, and fish chowder, New England Boiled Dinner (corned beef and boiled vegetables), Boston baked beans, and blueberry pie. In Louisiana, Creole specialties are blackened fish, shrimp gumbo, and Creole pralines. The West goes in for barbecued meats of any kind, corn-on-the-cob, baked trout, and bean soup. However, don't expect to automatically find New England specialties in New England restaurants, western specialties in the West, etc. You will probably have to search them out.

Bar Restaurants

Some of the better food is found in places where much drinking is done. It won't be fancy, but simple steaks and large sandwiches are often excellent and not overpriced. You do want to take the noise factor into consideration.

Trendy Restaurants

In many of these places, the chef dreams up original dishes, sometimes in the name of good health. "California Cuisine" has made a splash lately by putting unexpected ingredients together and cooking them with very little fat or cream. Trendy restaurants are the ones talked about, and "foodies" hasten to every new one. Certain regional cuisines periodically become trendy and fill up with fashionably dressed young people. Cajun (Louisiana/French) food is very modish right now, as are Thai and Cambodian restaurants. Trendy restaurants may play alarmingly loud and awful music by way of suggesting that they are fun places.

Haute Cuisine

The peak dining experiences in America are often in the French restaurants. This is also where you'll find the most intimidating level of service – captains, tuxedoed waiters, sommeliers, busboys, and so on. It is best to have an expense account and to know bits of French in order to read the menu.

You will need to make a reservation – by phone – in advance. If you don't arrive reasonably on time (within 15 minutes or so), you may not get a table. Some restaurants enjoy such popularity that they are booked weeks in advance.

There is a lot of rigmarole to eating in these places, and many Americans feel a bit insecure about protocol in them. When the waiter uncorks the wine, he will pour a little bit into the glass of whoever ordered it. This person is to taste it, and then nod approvingly, perhaps adding "very good," whereupon the waiter will serve the other members of the party. Some people also make a fuss about sniffing the cork, but the real experts say a bad cork doesn't prove anything.

You are only supposed to refuse the wine if it's actually not fit to drink – not because you have just discovered that you don't like that particular wine. This will only expose you as ignorant.

93

When the check comes, you should study the items and addition before paying. This is a very respectable thing to do, and you may be sure that even Rockefellers (the legendary rich American family) take care that they are not being overcharged.

Waiters in these grand places hope for 20% tips (very rarely is a tip already added to the bill); there's a place on the credit card receipt for adding a tip. Calculate tip on the pre-tax charge. Do not worry about tipping the many different individuals who served you, unless you had some special service, such as a maître d' who found you a table when you hadn't reserved one. A cloakroom attendant should be tipped a dollar per coat.

Not every French restaurant is so formal, and there are now plenty of other kinds of restaurants vying with the French ones for the top dollars; high-class Italian and "Continental" (eclectic European) are contenders and achieve similar degrees of elegance.

Drinking

Although Americans are consuming less alcohol than ever before, drinking still occupies a large role on the social stage. "Let's meet for a drink" usually means let's get together at a bar after work and before dinner, although such a thing can also be done after dinner.

Some bars serve food, but their primary stock is alcohol. The price of the same drink could vary from $1.00 in a down-and-out saloon to $6.00 in a mahogany-panelled room with a view. You won't get a menu, but the bartender is supposed to know how to make almost any concoction you order. Mixed drinks (known as cocktails when consumed before dinner) have ringing names that suggest little about the ingredients: martinis, margaritas, Tom & Jerry's, Bloody Mary's. Some of them pack a wallop so it's wise to find out what you're imbibing. You may also order whisky neat (no ice), on the rocks (with ice), or in a highball (with ice and water in a tall glass).

Don't let it worry you if you don't happen to drink. Many people do not and go right on "meeting for drinks." Soda water or tonic with lime are non-drinker standards, and every bartender can make a Virgin Mary – spicy tomato juice without the vodka of a Bloody Mary.

In some bars, you pay for your first round with a large bill, then leave the change on the counter. The bartender will remove the correct amount from the pile for each subsequent round. You pocket what's left when you're finished, leaving a tip.

After a few drinks, you do not wish to casually wander the streets of any large American city late at night. Be sure you know where you are and how you're getting home. And don't accept a ride from a friend who has had one drink too many.

TABLE MANNERS

When to Eat

Back on the farm, where the day started at 4 a.m., dinner was at 5 p.m. Our dinner hour remains quite early. You might meet someone at a restaurant anytime between 6 and 8, but rarely later, unless traveling in very sophisticated circles. The East Coast operates at somewhat later hours than the West, partly because people on the West Coast have to get up early in the morning to call people on the East Coast.

Breakfast takes place before the day's work begins, whenever that is. Noon is the classic lunch hour, although many people eat earlier or later – largely to escape the crowds. Few people take more than an hour for lunch, unless there's a business excuse for it.

The Mechanics of Eating

Correctly, no one should start eating until everyone has been served. However, if some people are served before others, the unserved should turn to the served and say, "Don't wait; please start." The served do so, but pick slowly at their food so that the others will be able to catch up.

A

B

C

A. Cutting with the knife and fork. One cuts only a few bites at a time.

B. Taking a bite: fork in action. Note that the eater leans slightly forward but does not slump over her plate.

C. The mouth closes daintily around the food. The diner continues to face her companion directly.

D. Eating soup, which the diner pours into her mouth from the side of the soup spoon.

E. When she senses that her lips are wet with food, the diner delicately wipes her mouth with her napkin.

F. This arrangement of knife and fork indicates to the waiter that the diner has not finished eating.

G. The arrangement of knife and fork here signals that the waiter may remove the plate.

Photos: Kristy MacDonald

The array of silverware at a classy dinner can be formidable, but the rule is simple: use it from the outside in. That is, you use the outside spoon for your soup, the middle one for dessert, and the inner one for your coffee. The truth is, though, that nobody will notice or care if you use the salad fork for your cake.

We eat nearly everything with a fork, which most right-handed people hold in the right hand. If something has to be cut up, you switch your knife to the right hand, do your cutting (holding the item in place with the fork in the left hand), then lay down the knife (on the side of the plate), switch the fork back to the right hand, stab the bite-sized piece with the fork and eat. Got it? There are those (English people in particular) who ridicule our mode, preferring the efficiency of keeping the fork in the left hand and the knife in the right.

You use the fork even when facing a number of foods that easily could be eaten with the fingers. Generally, if something could grease up your fingers, don't touch it. The exception is fried chicken, which may be seized between both hands. Bread, bacon, artichokes, pizza, olives, corn-on-the-cob, and raw vegetables may be eaten with the fingers. With rolls and muffins, we break off and butter one small piece at a time, having first transferred an adequate supply of butter from the general butter plate to our own butter plate. Never stick your hand or your fork into a serving dish. If you want the last cherry tomato left in the salad bowl, remove it to your plate with the salad tongs.

When the knife is not in action, it is most pleasing to have the free hand resting in the lap, although few people will look askance at a forearm on the table. The eating arm should rise off the table when carrying food to the mouth; the mouth must not be lowered to meet the fork or spoon. One leans forward slightly to avoid drips in one's lap. Elbows are properly kept off the table, at least until the plates are cleared. Implements should not be waved around in the air to punctuate the conversation.

Foods too liquid to be eaten with a fork are eaten with a spoon: soup, ice cream, puddings. It is bad form to drink from your soup bowl, which should not be lifted from the table. The soup spoon is slightly larger than a dessert or coffee spoon, and you pour its contents into your mouth from its side, not from the tip. When you're finished, lay the spoon on the plate under the soup bowl. You're not supposed to leave cutlery in a sticking-up position. You indicate that you've finished eating by laying the knife and fork side-by-side on the right-hand side of the plate.

You should not burp or slurp at the table, although blowing one's nose is perfectly all right. (Persistent sniffling is irritating.) Do not pick your teeth. Food should slide into your mouth as quietly as possible, then be chewed with the mouth closed. Our well-bred are quite repulsed by the sight of the food in someone else's mouth. Therefore, you must swallow your food before speaking or at least give the appearance of having done so. Should someone suddenly ask if you realize that your wife is having an affair, you must still finish chewing before replying.

The Check

My Chinese friend was dumbfounded to hear of a father and two brothers who went out to dinner and split the check three ways. I assured him that this was most unusual in a family, but among friends, splitting the check is common. Unless it was made very clear to you that someone else is paying – or you are – you should expect to pay your share of the check.

If you're with friends, and someone else grabs the check and says, "Here, I'll get this," you might protest, but you can generally assume the other person genuinely means to pay. If you really don't want him or her to, you can try to force a bill over, saying, "Here, at least take this," or offer to pay the tip.

A frequent question is whether to simply split the check in equal shares or have each person pay for precisely what she ate. The person who says, "Let's just split it, shall we?" should not be the one who consumed most extravagantly. So if you ordered filet mignon and insisted on champagne, you should pay more.

This exactitude horrifies many foreigners, but it represents not so much stinginess on our part as our fondness for self-reliance and our idea of fairness. If you don't owe me and I don't owe you, we have a nice even relationship (which I may be willing to sacrifice in favor of a free meal, but if I really doubt that you can afford to pick up the check, I will be embarrassed if you insist on paying).

Smoking Sections

Certain municipalities require restaurants to provide both smoking and non-smoking sections, and the hostess will ask you which you would prefer. When this question comes up, smokers do not automatically defer to non-smokers. If yours is a mixed party, you will just have to try to work out your seating in the way that will cause the least all-round suffering.

FREEDOM FROM DIRT

Home and Person

"Cleanliness is next to godliness," my grandmother used to say. Americans are almost religious in their devotion to eliminating dirt. Daily baths or showers are the norm, underwear and socks are changed daily, and men head out the door each morning in a fresh shirt.

In fact, it has been shown that the American housewife spends *more* time doing housework than she did fifty years ago. One reason is that standards of cleanliness have risen to meet the time saved by washing machines and vacuum cleaners. A great deal of effort can go into making kitchen floors and counters shine; supermarkets fill entire aisles with cleaning formulas and devices.

Most important of all, the American person does not wish to smell dirty. The matter is so sensitive that hardly anyone will tell someone who smells bad the truth. An enormous industry produces deodorants, after-shave lotions, powders, and colognes guaranteed to fend off any hint of body odor. A person who vigorously exercises will want to shower immediately afterwards. Houses now often have as many or more bathrooms as occupants, each a sparkling temple to cleanliness.

The Streets

On a world scale, American cities aren't too dirty, but they don't compete with Copenhagen or Tokyo. We do not like garbage-strewn streets, and the better suburbs are immaculate, with perfectly cut lawns and not an ice cream wrapper in sight. In many poor city neighborhoods, on the other hand, trash blows around freely, and graffiti defeat fresh-paint efforts.

Under no circumstances should you drop waste – be it ever so small – on the ground. Practically every community has some sort of public trash collection, but we are a civic-minded people and consider everyone responsible for keeping the outdoors tidy. If there is no trash can in sight, you may have to fill your pockets with empty bottles and candy wrappers until you get home. Good citizens go so far as to pick up other people's refuse when they're in a park or garden.

The rule goes for the middle of the desert, the national parks, zoos, and mountaintops as well. Those who offend nature by leaving refuse behind are considered to have had derelict upbringings. Alas, there are many of them, despite fines for littering. In a country like ours, which generates such mountains of waste, one considers with horror where general littering would lead.

Noise Pollution

As might be expected in a country settled by Pilgrims, Puritans, and Quakers, we don't like unnecessary noise. We can stand the sounds of progress such as jackhammers and chainsaws, but we do not feel our neighbor has the right to disturb our peace.

At any rate, this is the opinion of the old guard. Unfortunately, our neighbor now has the means at his disposal – namely stereos with incredible decibel levels – to disturb us from blocks away. Since popular music has come to rely on volume to impose its message viscerally, a generation has grown up that seems to equate silence with death. But it should not be thought that because some excuse for music is everywhere, filling elevators and offices, that everybody loves it. Primarily it is the idea of youth to live in a world where the music never stops, and, as many foreigners have ob-served, the power of youth has gone out of hand in the USA. It is often necessary to find a very expensive restaurant in order to dine in peace.

Noise and the Law

Despite the inroads of the noisy, the law is generally on the side of the peaceful. Each community has its own noise code, regulating volumes at certain times of day and night. If your neighbors continuously disturb you with noisy parties, you can probably get satisfaction by calling the police – and many people do (to the horror of my friend from El Salvador who can't imagine doing such a thing to one's neighbors). Driving around blasting a car stereo is strictly illegal in most cities, although police are preoccupied with other matters.

If you have neighbors whose television or stereo disturbs you, you should not be embarrassed to ask them to turn it down. You will be performing a community service. One is often successful in requesting a reduction of musical volume in restaurants.

Some suburban areas have banned the use of leaf blowers because their roar filled every weekend. If you find yourself in a backyard community, you might consider what you can do to preserve the quiet. The soothing click-click of a manual lawnmower is much more pleasant than the roar of a gas-powered one.

Theaters, Concerts, Churches

There are countries where chatter by members of the audience does not cause offense, but this isn't one of them. Here, any movement of the lips is thought to be too much – and that includes during the overture. Also no unwrapping of cough drops, excessive coughing (leave if you must), cracking of joints, chewing gum, foot-tapping, jingling jewelry, or undue fidgeting. The general feeling is, "I paid as much for my ticket as you did and I'm not bothering you so what right have you to interfere with my enjoyment of this concert/opera/show?"

The rules for the movies are slightly less strict, but still commentary should not extend beyond a whispered, "I'll be right back." Noisy unwrapping of candy bars, etc. will produce dirty looks from those around you.

Smoking

Smoking is very much out of fashion in the United States. As soon as smoke from other people's cigarettes ("second-hand smoke") was proven unhealthy, the non-smokers drew battle lines. There is now a ban on radio and television advertising of cigarettes. Smoking is prohibited on all airline flights within the Continental United States. Ordinances have passed in many locales banning all smoking in public buildings. Many restaurants have smoking and non-smoking sections. Some companies don't allow smoking; others have incentive programs to get their employees to quit.

A smoker may reach for a cigarette with some embarrassment. It is generally assumed that he is someone who has tried to quit and failed; by smoking he reveals some flaw in his personality. If you wish nonetheless to smoke, first make sure you're doing it in a place you're allowed to. Do not ever light up in an elevator (fire regulations prohibit).

If you're in someone's home or office, before getting out your cigarettes you should ask, "Does anyone mind if I smoke?" If nobody does, your host should produce an ashtray for you. (If, however, there are ashtrays conspicuously about, you may assume smoking is approved.) Some people have gone so far as to put little bronze plaques on their coffee tables which say, "Thank you for not smoking."

If your need is great, you can always step outdoors into the street for a smoke. House guests of non-smokers may spend a good deal of time in the garden.

Pipe smoking is slightly more acceptable than cigarette smoking, but pipe smokers should still inquire before lighting up. Cigar smoking is simply unacceptable indoors unless you and your host are alone smoking cigars together.

Driving

An international driver's license, available at American Automobile Association (AAA) offices, is a desirable item to have, but not absolutely required for visitors. However, the police would much rather deal with one than something in, say, Arabic and so would rental car companies. You must get an American driver's license after a year's residence here, which requires passing both a written and a driver's test. Even if your stay won't be that long, it's a good idea to pick up a booklet on driving rules at the state motor vehicle bureau.

Traffic laws are taken seriously here. While it's true that on some highways marked at 55 miles per hour the traffic may be moving at 65 miles per hour, the argument that "everybody was doing it" will not help you in court. You must come to a complete stop at red lights and stop signs, even if there isn't another car in sight (the one you don't see may be a police car).

Highway patrolmen are honest so don't try to bribe them. If you have been speeding, the officer will write you a ticket, which you will have several weeks to pay.

If a police car wants to stop you, he will follow you flashing his overhead lights. Even if you can't imagine what's on his mind, pull over. You should remain in your car, with your driver's license and car registration ready. You may also need to produce proof of car insurance.

Parking regulations are enforced as well, and fines can be high. It is particularly dispiriting to find that one's car has been towed away and can only be retrieved at great cost. You will have to find out what the various curb colors and signs in different communities indicate. Never park in front of a fire hydrant or at a bus stop. In most states, you may make a right turn on a red light, traffic permitting.

Do not attempt to bribe a policeman. The gesture will not be appreciated, and happily, corruption among them is low. You might do better trying to persuade one that your foreignness accounted for your confusion. If you feel you have been unfairly cited, you may appear in traffic court and argue your case.

HAZARDS

Crime

Few people arrive here unaware of American crime. It is so well publicized that many foreigners are surprised to find that there isn't a bandit behind every tree. Although there is indeed a high crime rate – which inhibits us all – the odds are that the visitor will not have any personal experience with it.

There are more than 20,000 murders a year in the USA. That means an inhabitant of this country has about one chance in 12,000 of being bumped off in one year. But the truth is that a high proportion of those murders take place in very poor neighborhoods or in criminal circles. Unless you're smuggling drugs, your odds of getting murdered are slight.

Nonetheless, slight odds are worse than none. I have not personally known any homicide victims, but when at home I am careful to bolt my front door, and I am cautious when walking in certain areas. There are districts of many cities that I would not set foot in under any circumstances.

Theft is a matter one quite realistically must take into consideration. Nearly everyone I know has been robbed at one time or another. The resulting misfortune is that we all must carry weighty key rings, locking ourselves in and out wherever we go. A vast amount of effort and money goes into guarding ourselves, our possessions, and our children – all to the detriment of civic life.

Many of us fantasize about going and living in one of the small towns in America where doors and windows are still left unlocked.

The Problem

A large proportion of crime is in some way related to illegal drugs. Drug use is widespread; users may be the disaffected offspring of middle-class families, but most often they are poor people, condemned to watch on television the ritzy lives of the successful.

The heaviest drug use is in the ghettos (city areas of much crime, little family stability, high unemployment) among hopeless young people. The drugs and the milieu in which they are taken dissolve moral compunctions, and brutal crimes result.

The crime problem is exacerbated by the millions of guns floating around the country. It is an amazing fact that almost anyone can go into a store and buy a handgun, or perhaps a semi-automatic machine gun.

A phrase in the United States Constitution granting the "right to bear arms" causes the National Rifle Association to insist that any limitation on gun sales is unconstitutional. Actually, the founding fathers were providing protection against unpopular tyrants and probably would have considered the free sales of handguns as crazy as most foreigners do.

Precautions

Foreigners are automatically more vulnerable to crime than natives because they're on unfamiliar territory. They are less aware of what trouble feels like, less wary of the suspicious character. They pause when they should be walking briskly and stare at the tops of buildings when they should be looking at doorways.

107

Here are a few precautions:

- Keep your wits about you. When you're on city streets, don't ever get so lost in rapture that you are not conscious of your surroundings. People who look lost in any manner are easy targets.
- In American cities, bad areas and good ones can be intermixed in a manner perilous to the stroller. If you're a visitor, have someone tell you which areas to avoid. If you suddenly find yourself in an uncomfortable area, leave, hailing a taxi if necessary.
- If someone asks you for money in a threatening manner, walk quickly by. It's perfectly all right to give to most panhandlers, but certain ones want your whole wallet rather than a quarter, and they intend to take the wallet forcibly once you get it out.
- Don't ever become separated from your pocketbook. You should have body contact with it at all times in public. Even in a restaurant, be sure you've stowed it where no one can snitch it. Mine was once lifted from under my table with an umbrella handle.
- Men's wallets are best in a sealed pocket. Lacking that, the front pants pocket or inside jacket pocket is best. Be on the lookout for anyone who jostles you in a crowd. (Sometimes he's just distracting you while his accomplice picks your pocket.)
- Don't carry around any more cash than you need. Nearly every purchase can be made with a credit card, and travelers' checks can provide cash reserves. The Japanese, who are not accustomed to paying for meals with credit cards and often carry large amounts of cash, are known to thieves as fine targets.
- Always lock your car. Put possessions in the trunk rather than visibly on car seats. If you're traveling with a carload of stuff, be careful where you park. At night bring bags into your motel or hotel. In some areas you don't even want to leave things in the trunk. People in New York City go so far as to put signs in their car windows, saying, "Thieves, don't bother. Radio already stolen."
- Don't wear good jewelry on bad streets. Even a gold chain on the streets of New York tempts fate.
- In hotels, have your valuables locked in the safe.

- Don't ever take your eyes off your luggage at an airport. Airports are well-worked by thieves, and foreigners are first-choice victims.
- Don't go to a park at night – unless there's some sort of event going on.
- If someone does "mug" you (threaten you with harm unless you turn over your money), give him your money. Far better to lose your money than to be hurt.
- Always lock hotel room, apartment, and house doors. Do not open the door unless you know who is on the other side. Many doors have a peephole so you can look through and see for yourself.
- If you open a window, check to make sure it doesn't provide easy access to an intruder. Close windows before going out.
- Have your keys ready before you walk into your building. If you are entering a locked apartment building, do not allow anyone to slip in with you. If you are entering the foyer of your building and think someone is following you, walk on down the street until you've lost the person.
- If you are robbed, call the police. In most areas, the police emergency number is 911. You do not pay the police for coming.

   This crime awareness becomes second nature after a little while, and soon you won't even notice how careful you've become.

Drugs

Illegal drugs have been a problem for a long time among the have-nots of America. Heroin (made from the poppy and imported from Asia and Latin America) has created drug addicts and caused crime for years. Marijuana has been long available in some inner city neighborhoods, but it was not until the 1960's that college students widely indulged in smoking marijuana. Since then, marijuana use has spread around the country.

Marijuana, which comes from an easily grown plant, makes the user feel dreamy and confused, passive rather than violent. For people who are "stoned" a lot, problems don't get solved, the laundry doesn't get washed, appointments aren't met. Its use is particularly unfortunate among young people who don't face the problems of growing up. It is a dangerous drug for a worker who must be alert. Fortunately, not everybody likes the effects of marijuana. Some people feel paranoid when they smoke it or unpleasantly weird.

Cocaine became very popular in the 1970's when it was falsely believed to be non-addictive. It was widely used by young, urban professionals because besides producing a fine feeling of well-being, it makes the user feel creative and energetic. However, the euphoria lasts but a short time, it's expensive, and people who became addicted are subject to some unpleasant physical side effects. Clinics are now full of people trying to kick the cocaine habit.

Cocaine comes from leaves of the coca plant, which is grown primarily in South America. It can be further refined into crack, a substance which when smoked provides a very fast high. Crack addicts appear to be the most desperate of all drug users. Babies born to crack or cocaine-addicted mothers often have multiple, and probably permanent, problems.

Amphetamines are synthetic stimulants, known as "speed." They inspire tremendous energy; users may stay awake for days at a time. Depression and even psychosis follows. These drugs are very debilitating and cause bizarre behavior.

LSD is a synthetic drug that induces hallucinations and thought disorders.

Just Say No

Every elected or appointed official is conscious of the monumental drug problem in America. The cure is elusive. There are programs to teach children to Just Say No To Drugs, drug rehabilitation programs, and federal attempts to intercept drugs before they reach the street. Obviously, none of this has been very successful as yet.

Despite the availability of drugs in schools, you should not worry excessively that your children will fall in with bad friends and start taking drugs. Although it's possible, if they are mature and well-directed, they are most unlikely to become steady users.

Alcohol

The most used drug is the legal one – alcohol. The first settlers were very heavy drinkers, and this has long been a hard-drinking country. Recently the consumption of alcohol has dropped, but alcohol still (it is estimated) contributes to over half the crimes committed and most certainly creates a great deal of unhappiness. Many families have someone who drinks too much in them, complete with neglected children and lost jobs.

Alcoholics rarely can stop drinking without help, which is available through Alcoholics Anonymous (AA), a worldwide group of sober alcoholics who give up drinking and stay sober by meeting together and helping each other. A listing for AA can be found in nearly every phonebook in the country. There are also many treatment programs for alcoholics.

In the past few years, public opinion has turned against the drinking driver, and people are more careful than they used to be about mixing automobiles and alcohol. Drunk driving laws have become quite strict; in many states you automatically lose your license if convicted. If you cause harm, you could go to jail for a long period of time.

If you are stopped by the police and accused of driving "under the influence," you must take the sobriety test offered, or you will be automatically convicted. The test will be of your breath, blood, or urine.

Medical Care

There is no national health plan in the USA, and the cost of medical care is staggering. Consequently, you must have private medical insurance. Insurance is costly, but without it illness could ruin you financially. A private room in a New York City hospital can cost $900 a day.

In fact, if you don't have insurance, you could be refused admission to a hospital (unless your situation is life-threatening in which case the nearest hospital has to take you) and have to go to the overcrowded public hospital – where you will still have to pay, unless you have no money whatsoever.

The medical profession charges up and down the line for each separate service – for X-rays, tests, medicines, and office visits; in addition to your hospital bill you may owe money to surgeons, anesthesiologists, private nurses, respiratory therapists, pharmacies, and people you scarcely realized existed. You will discover a charge for each time your doctor popped into your room and nodded his head.

Getting Insurance

If you are working for a company here, your employer will probably provide paid health insurance, but note that policies rarely cover all medical expenses. If you don't have employee insurance, you will have to find a private plan, and your travel agent should be able to advise you on short-term insurance. Colleges have health plans for students.

The poor aren't completely without resources. Medi-Care, a national plan, provides coverage for the old and disabled; various state plans cover the indigent. Often, the out-of-luck are those working in jobs too marginal to provide medical insurance. And nearly everybody is out of luck except the very rich if long-term care is required because few insurance policies cover nursing homes.

Quality of Care

At its best, American medical care is excellent, and people come from all over the world to have esoteric operations and advanced cancer treatment. In most hospitals your care will be more than adequate, although nurses are extremely busy and rarely linger by your bedside.

As in most countries, it's helpful to have family or friends around to assist with your more mundane needs. However, you will find American hospital wards very quiet. The presumption here is that the sick person needs to rest and to rest he or she has to be alone. So large gatherings at the bedside are rare. Friends arrive with flowers, but make their visits very brief. An alternative to visiting is to send a get-well card or to have a florist make up and deliver a bouquet of flowers to the hospital.

You may find that for a simple ailment you are offered much more extensive and high-technology care than you would get in your own country. This is partly because doctors get sued if they don't consider every possible permutation of a problem. You can refuse treatment that you don't want; if some test or treatment seems extreme, talk over the alternatives with the doctor.

Up-to-date American doctors are encouraged not to be too bossy or domineering and are supposed to be happy to discuss your problems at length – it's considered desirable for patients to understand what is happening to them. Because the doctor shortage is over, patients can afford to walk away from a doctor who is curt or rude.

Very few doctors make house calls; no matter how sick you are you will be expected to appear in their offices unless you are in the

113

hospital. A recognized problem is that in this world of specialists there may be nobody who is in charge of your case. The latest specialty is that of "family medicine" – the doctor who coordinates the specialists.

It's a good idea to line up a doctor – if not a "family" specialist, perhaps an internist, as soon as you arrive if you're staying for an extended period. If anything bad happens, you will need a doctor to admit you to a hospital. Furthermore, most effective drugs – antibiotics for instance – must be prescribed by doctors. So there's a good chance you'll be wanting a doctor sooner or later. If you cannot get recommendations from friends, local medical societies are glad to give you names.

Mainstream Alternatives

A segment of the population has become increasingly skeptical about modern medicine, which often seems to have lost touch with human and spiritual forces. Occasionally the treatment is worse than the disease, and the reluctance on the part of both doctors and patients to let nature take its course leads to an over-medicated population.

In reaction, people both have started looking after themselves (through diet, exercise, etc.) and have turned to "alternative" health practitioners: acupuncturists, homeopaths, chiropractors (who do not consider themselves "alternative"), nutritionists, Chinese herbalists, and other healers. Time-honored native remedies are much in vogue among the avant-garde. Most of the aforementioned healers have the advantage of being fairly harmless, if not helpful. But do not assume that because they operate legally there is reason to believe that their cures work. It's strictly *caveat emptor* (Latin for "let the buyer beware") in this department – which admittedly is the case no matter what kind of doctor is treating you.

AIDS

AIDS (Acquired Immune Deficiency Disease) has reached epidemic proportions in parts of the USA. It is a tragic disease, striking down many young and wonderful people. The majority of the sufferers are either homosexual men or drug addicts who have shared needles.

You need not worry about contracting AIDS unless a) you have sexual relations with someone who carries the virus, b) you shoot drugs with dirty needles, or c) you receive infected blood in a blood transfusion. The blood supply is tested for the AIDS virus, but the test is not definitive so it is best not to have a transfusion unless absolutely necessary.

If you feel you must have sexual relations with someone who could carry the AIDS virus, you should use a latex condom. But condoms can fail and are no guarantee of safety. Drug addicts and homosexuals are the likeliest AIDS carriers, but heterosexuals are not exempt. The days of exuberant free love in America are over.

The chaste visitor will also protect himself or herself from a few other venereal diseases – herpes, syphilis, gonorrhea – that would be unpleasant to take home.

Do not take up with prostitutes – male or female. Other than in a few counties in the state of Nevada, prostitution is illegal in the USA. Consequently, prostitutes are not subject to disease checks, and many are drug addicts. Furthermore, you could end up being beaten and robbed. The sexual underworld is no place for an amateur.

Suing

The practice of dragging one's neighbor, doctor, spouse, host, and employer into court causes shock among newcomers to this country. We are a most litigious people, and we prefer to believe that there is always a responsible party for every event in life.

People have sued for: injuries attained while breaking into houses, losing a spelling bee, being fired, loss of pleasure when injured, emotional distress, tripping on sidewalks, and choking in restaurants.

The list of seemingly ridiculous suits provides great mirth and sometimes large awards.

To some degree, the pattern of suing has led to safer places and practices, but to a greater extent it has created high insurance rates and the sacrifice of services. Towns have gone bankrupt when held responsible for accidents on public property. Schools have lost play yards because they can't afford liability insurance. Some churches won't shelter the homeless because they lack the necessary insurance.

Bad as the situation is, some foreigners have picked up an even exaggerated idea of it. It is not true that no doctor will ever stop if there's an accident. In many states, a "good Samaritan" law forbids suing a doctor under such circumstances. Families still take friends' children camping. Usually if your friend falls off your garden wall and plans to sue you, he will find out what your insurance is first and the suit can be worked out amicably without much damage to you. Nonetheless, if someone could break a leg falling through the hole on your front porch, fix it.

Should you decide to do a little suing yourself, bear in mind that it's one thing to sue and win, another to collect. It's not worth the bother of going to court unless you have a realistic chance of seeing the money. Much of the proceeds of a case often end up in the lawyers' hands. Cases drag on for years, and your time will be unpleasantly spent. The two parties to the dispute usually, in one way or another, both lose.

Homelessness

Most immigrants no longer arrive thinking the streets of America will be paved with gold, but neither do they expect to find people sleeping in the streets. This is still the world's richest country. But people live on the streets, by the hundreds, in all the major cities. Thousands more spend nights in temporary shelters, not knowing where they're going to spend the following nights.

America has a housing problem. In the last twenty years, little low-cost housing has been built, and rents and house prices have climbed dizzyingly. What used to be cheap housing is now expensive. It is a much greater struggle than it used to be for a reasonably successful family to afford a house; for marginal people it becomes impossible.

A proportion of the people living on the streets are beyond helping themselves. But an increasing number of the homeless are families or single mothers with children. Some of these have just had a run of bad luck, and others have problems exacerbated by drugs, alcohol, or mental instability. Clearly, the looseness of family ties is a factor – otherwise more of those down on their luck would have a relative to stay with. There are teenagers living on the streets because they have run away or been kicked out of an abusive home.

Foreigners find the homeless situation difficult to comprehend because often in their own countries – no matter how poor – everybody still has a place to stay even if shared with many others. Here, both city governments and private charities try to provide shelters for everybody, but there is never enough money. The homeless situation is a new dilemma for America, and one we are all ashamed of.

Chapter Seven

GOD AND COUNTRY

Motherhood, God, and the Flag. Any United States politician who hopes to be re-elected must take these three sacred icons seriously. While most foreigners will easily comprehend the tributes paid to motherhood, the attitude to religion remains confusing to many and that towards the flag mystifying.

In God We Trust

The American viewpoint on religion is paradoxical. We honor the separation of Church and State (and the freedom to worship at the church of one's choice), but in public life few people dare admit to having no religious belief at all.

The Supreme Court keeps watch over freedom of religion – prayer is not allowed in schools, or (thanks to a recent court decision) at the beginning of football games. Religion is supposed to be a private matter, between the individual, his conscience, and his church.

Nonetheless, there is a widespread feeling that decent people believe in God and that ethical standards spring from religion. Politicians frequently assure the electorate of their faith in God. The President may begin his State of the Union message with a supplication to God, and when asked what he would do in a crisis, our Vice President said his first move would be to pray.

Our coins all have "In God We Trust" cast on them; the Pledge of Allegiance to the Flag calls us "one nation, under God." Presumably, some of this religiosity is left over from the religious orientation of early America. Religious cults have been prominent through our history. Religious belief jibes with American optimism and the faith that justice will prevail, if not in this world, then in the next.

The Christian Majority

It's the Christian God that most people have in mind when they invoke Him. In the United States, 85% of the population describe themselves as Christians; 2% are Jewish, 4% are "other" – Buddhist, various Eastern religions, Moslems, etc. – and 9% claim no religion. The only national religious holidays are Christian holidays. However, employers must respect the demands of anyone's religion and grant absences when religion requires it.

Three out of four Americans claim to believe in God, and four out of ten go to church regularly. On the other hand, foreigners shouldn't imagine that the average American is deeply involved with his religion. We only expect our leaders to have some faith in God, not to take their religion more seriously than their golf games.

Sectarianism

A majority (57%) of Americans are Protestants – Christians who do

119

Photo: Esther Wanning

Parishioners linger to chat after church on Sunday morning. With the idea of showing respect in "God's house," people usually dress up to go to church.

not follow the Church of Rome (Catholicism). As Protestants have no central authority, there are hundreds of denominations. All adhere to one God and the Bible, differently interpreted. Some churches have very dignified services, whereas others involve a lot of emotional display. As a general rule, it's the dignified ones (Episcopalian, Congregational, Presbyterian) that are the more upper class, and many a rising salesman has switched from the Baptist to the Episcopalian Church when he moved to a better neighborhood.

The remaining Christians are Catholics (28%), a group by and large reflecting Irish, Italian, and South American immigration. The Catholics have known discrimination and even (unjustifiably) have been suspected of dividing their allegiances between the Roman pope and their country. Until the election of John F. Kennedy, many people thought that no Catholic could ever win the presidency.

Besides the established religions, there are numerous religious cults. Most cults are dependent on the charisma of the leader and don't outlast him or her. An Englishman I know suggests that the way to get rich in America is to start a religion. Cults demand a wholehearted commitment from the followers, and scandals erupt among them frequently.

Various Hindu and Buddhist leaders have attracted significant followings in recent years. Some of these leaders are learned messengers from the East, and others acquire power and wealth, while making a little learning go a long way.

"Born Agains"

The "Born Again Christians" are the most surprising among today's religious sects. Not long ago, intellectuals assumed that now that science had explained most phenomena, belief in God could not last much longer. They were very wrong. Instead, millions of people have joined a variety of fundamentalist groups. These people are collectively called "Born Agains" because they believe that their lives started anew when they committed themselves to Jesus Christ.

They hold the Bible, despite its contradictions, to be literally true – which leads to the problem of evolution.

Darwin or Adam

The Bible says that God made the world and the first man and woman (Adam and Eve) in six days. (On the seventh, he rested, which is why Sunday is supposed to be a day of rest among Christians.) If this is true, the theory of evolution, as described by Charles Darwin, must be wrong. So say the fundamentalists. The evolutionists say that man evolved over millions of years.

The evidence is strongly on the side of Darwin, but there are people who persist in believing that the Bible is literally true; there are actually states in which teachers are compelled to teach both sides. Over this issue, many fundamentalists have withdrawn their children from public schools altogether and enrolled them in Christian schools.

The fundamentalists are not usually highly educated and are strongest in the south. It seems likely that their rise comes from the tempting desire amid the confusion of modern life to return to a simpler society. Fundamentalist preachers can be seen on many cable television stations, and visitors should make a point of tuning in at least once. However, they should not make the mistake of thinking these preachers represent mainstream thinking.

Abortion

The other big issue that brings out religious divisions is abortion. Presently, in most states, any woman who so desires may have an abortion, but there is a strong movement (called "Right to Life") to make abortion illegal. The campaign against abortion is rooted in the religious belief that all human life is sacred and begins at conception, but many feminists think that the real root is the desire to keep women subservient and pregnant.

The Catholic Church considers contraception as well as abortion

Photo: The Weekly Packet

This man, bowing his head in prayer at the annual Blessing of the Fleet in a coastal town in Maine, is prompting his dog to bow its head in prayer too.

immoral. However, Catholic women practice birth control as much as other American women do.

Charities

Judeo-Christian values emphasize the importance of aiding the poor and unfortunate. Many of the hungry are fed from church basements, and some of the country's largest charities are administered by a

123

church group. Hospitals, homeless shelters, workshops for the disabled, schools, teen centers, and countless other projects are church or synagogue-supported – although often run without any overt religious overtones.

The majority of Americans donate to charities, for everything from saving the forests to medical research. Some people even have contributions deducted from their paychecks.

The Flag

Patriotism comes close to being a religion in America. Patriots demonstrate their love of America and freedom through respect for the flag. Politicians make a great furor over loving the flag. In the course of the 1988 election, the House of Representatives elected to prove its patriotism by voting to salute the flag every morning. Few representatives were brave enough to vote against this silly exercise.

Citizens of other countries pay homage to their flags too, but the belligerence with which Americans proclaim their patriotism is surprising to outsiders. In many countries, to insist that your country is the best country in the world is unpleasantly chauvinistic. But Americanism means believing America is a special nation chosen by God.

Professional sports events begin with singing the national anthem (whereupon men take their hats off and some people put their hands on their hearts), and the flag waves above all government offices. Although the Supreme Court has ruled that the right to burn the flag is protected, there are still laws on the books (mostly unenforced) about bringing the flag in after dark, not wearing it, and not trampling upon it.

Many schools begin each day with the students standing up, facing the flag, and with their hands on their hearts, saying "I pledge allegiance to the flag of the United States of America and to the Republic for which it stands – one nation, under God, indivisible, with liberty and justice for all."

Chapter Eight

EDUCATION

It is largely by passing through our public school system that immigrant families from all over the world have come to identify themselves as thoroughly American, registering American values, culture, and folklore. Without this educational filter, it's doubtful if the American experiment could have worked.

American public schools provide free schooling to every child from ages 5 to 18 – or from kindergarten through 12th grade. Because each of the fifty states runs its own schools, school requirements vary across the nation, and there is no federal testing of students. In most states, attendance is mandatory until age 16.

The Educational Prescription

The object of the American school system is to bestow a broad education on every youngster. This is not an overly ambitious goal. Only a few students are expected to become intellectuals or scholars. The rest we hope will be able to read, write, think, and deal with the issues of the day. In keeping with the democracy principle, there are no absolute turning points when a crucial exam separates the sheep from the goats. Theoretically, anyone who completes the academic school course is college material.

Problems

Currently, our schools are a source of intense distress because many of our younger citizens, despite 13 continuous years' school attendance, are profoundly ignorant. Few know where Alaska is, what the Bill of Rights is, when the Civil War was fought, or who Thomas Jefferson was. One of my friends, the principal of an exclusive private school, discovered to his chagrin that not one of his 8th graders had any idea what the circumference of the world might be.

One out of four students does not graduate from high school and too many of those who do can barely read and know next to nothing of the world. In a recent six-nation survey of schoolchildren's mathematics and science skills, the Americans scored dead last in mathematics, and almost last in science.

It appears that a large number of our schoolchildren have few facts and little thinking ability at their command. Whether this is solely the fault of the schools or whether parental irresponsibility, television, drugs, and family breakdown, etc., are equally to blame is the subject of great debate.

Concern about the educational system is nearly always couched in terms of national needs. If the next generation can't read, who will run the businesses? If they can't compute, how will we compete with the Japanese and the Russians?

Education for its own sake, for the sheer love of knowledge, does not get much press. Education, like everything else in America, must be justified in practical terms.

Educational Philosophy

For the past fifty years our schools have operated on the theories of John Dewey (1859–1952), an American educator and writer. Dewey believed that the school's job was to enhance the natural development of the growing child, rather than to pour information, for which the child had no context, into him or her. In the Dewey system, the child becomes the active agent in his own education, rather than a passive receptacle for facts.

Consequently, American schools are very enthusiastic about teaching "life skills" – logical thinking, analysis, creative problem-solving. The actual content of the lessons is secondary to the process, which is supposed to train the child to be able to handle whatever life may present, including all the unknowns of the future. Students and teachers both regard pure memorization as uncreative and somewhat vulgar.

In addition to "life skills," schools are assigned to solve the ever-growing stock of social problems. Racism, teenage pregnancy, alcoholism, drug use, reckless driving, and suicide are just a few of the modern problems that have appeared on the school curriculum. This all contributes to a high degree of social awareness in American youngsters.

School Structure

At the age of five, children start kindergarten, where they concentrate on getting ready for the heavier burdens of grade school by singing songs, painting pictures, learning to hang up their coats, and identifying numbers and letters. Grades 1 through 5 or 6 are known as elementary or grade school, and at the very least teach reading, writing, and arithmetic, along with varying degrees of art, gym (sports), social studies, and science. The curriculum usually broadens in middle school/junior high (which can be anything from 5th to 8th grades to just 7th and 8th grades), and by high school (which traditionally begins with 9th grade) a wide choice of elective courses may be offered – including such unacademic subjects as car repair, typing, homemaking, and art.

Those in their first year of high school, 9th grade, are called freshmen; 10th graders are sophomores; 11th graders are juniors; and 12th graders are seniors. (This terminology repeats itself in college when first-year students are freshmen; second-year students are sophomores, etc.)

Student Life

To the students, the most notable difference between elementary school and the higher levels is that in junior high they start "changing classes." This means that rather than spending the day in one classroom, they switch classrooms to meet their different teachers. This gives them three or four minutes between classes in the hallways, where a great deal of the important social action of high school traditionally takes place. Students have lockers in these hallways, around which they congregate.

Society in general does not take the business of studying very seriously. Schoolchildren have a great deal of free time, which they are encouraged to fill with extracurricular activities – sports, clubs, cheerleading, scouts – supposed to inculcate such qualities as leadership, sportsmanship, ability to organize, etc. Those who don't become engaged in such activities or have after-school jobs have plenty of opportunity to "hang out," listen to teenage music, and watch television.

Compared to other nations, American students do not have much homework. Studies also show that American parents have lower expectations for their children's success in school than other nationalities do. (Historically, there has not been much correlation

EDUCATION

Photo: The Weekly Packet

*Cub scouts at a Memorial Day parade. Cub scouts and the
older boy scouts take an oath to be "trustworthy, loyal, helpful,
friendly, courteous, kind, obedient, cheerful, thrifty, brave,
clean, and reverent."*

between American school success and success in later life.) "He's
just not a scholar," the American parents might say, content that
their son is on the swim team and doesn't take drugs. (Some of the
young do choose to study hard, for reasons of their own, such as
determining that the road to riches lies through Harvard Business
School.)

What American schools do effectively teach is the competitive method. In innumerable ways children are pitted against each other – whether in classroom discussion, spelling bees, reading groups, or tests. Every classroom is expected to produce a scattering of A's and F's (teachers often grade A=excellent; B=good; C=average; D=poor; and F=failed). A teacher who gives all A's looks too soft – so students are aware that they are competing for the limited number of top marks.

Foreign students sometimes don't understand that copying from other people's papers or from books is considered wrong and taken seriously. Here, it is important to show that you have done your own work and are displaying your own knowledge. It is more important than helping your friends to pass, whom we think do not deserve to pass unless they can provide their own answers. Group effort goes against the competitive grain, and American students do not study together as many Asians do. Many Asians in this country consider their group study habits a large contributor to their school success.

The Ever-Blowing Winds of Change

Sadly, the current school situation caps twenty years of well-intentioned reform. The progressivism of the sixties was successful in making school curriculums more sensitive to the cultures of students not of the white, Christian majority. Most of the old textbooks were jettisoned as being too sexist and ethnocentric. In the last twenty years there has been a massive attempt to integrate the school system so that Black, Hispanic, Asian, etc. students would mix with other groups. The term "busing" refers to the practice of transporting students by bus out of one neighborhood into another in order to balance racial groups.

Unfortunately, one response to busing was for many white people to move to suburban towns – or to send their children to private schools. Today, many urban schools don't have very many white students left to add to the racial mix.

The ideals of the 1960's also included a thrust towards "relevance" in education – even more lively exploration by the students, even less memorization. A great democratization blew through the schools, and the subject of students' rights was taken very seriously. Dress codes were thrown out, required subjects became few, a teacher's word was no longer law. If students could be themselves and pursue their own interests – went the thinking – then they'd get a real education.

The wind is blowing the other way now. Admirable as the ideology sounded, the fruit has not been a crop of inspired, self-motivated students. Instead, test scores sank, disrespect for teachers fell to a new low, discipline became the number one problem in many schools, and students' own interests led more often in the direction of drugs than towards intellectual endeavor.

The Cure

When and where our school system works, it provides the means for someone from the poorest home to advance in society. It clearly works less well now than formerly, and a number of theorists have turned up to explain why.

One of these is E.D. Hirsch, Jr., the author of the bestselling book, *Cultural Literacy*. Hirsch concludes that our nation is in peril because students are no longer being taught the shared information that bonds Americans together. Furthermore, he posits, one cannot be literate exclusive of information. Reading, writing, and thinking, he says, depend on a wide range of specific information.

Currently, only two-thirds of our citizenry are genuinely literate, and these at a lower level than should be acceptable. And so, he concludes (and many agree), the sooner we get away from the "skills model" of education and on with teaching something real the better.

Hirsch's book includes a list of 5,000 of the names, phrases, dates, and concepts he regards as essential for cultural literacy in the

USA. The list, although controversial, should be informative for any foreigner. (A sampling of A's: abolitionism, abstract art, AFL/CIO, andante, Aristotle, Fred Astaire, atom, Aztecs.)

Teacher Respect

Teaching is not a high-status occupation in the United States. This is in keeping with the pay scale, which is poor compared to other professions. (In another country, one could be respected and poor, but rarely in America.) Furthermore, teaching has traditionally been a woman's field, another strike against it. And in all truth, many teachers are not well-educated, having frequently been trained in teaching methods rather than in an academic field.

Teachers are treated shabbily inside as well as outside the schools. They are seen as the foot soldiers who must carry out the constant flow of orders descending from school boards, politicians, principals, and parents. Every year, in the worst schools, teachers are injured by students. Students' rights remain paramount, and teachers must be prepared to justify their actions in all matters.

Many foreigners have rather simplistically concluded that it's the absence of corporal punishment (which is illegal in many states) in the schools that causes all the problems, but few Americans would agree. To Americans, corporal punishment is unfair, giving too much power to the strong.

School Choices

All this is not to say that every school is a jungle. Although there are abysmal schools, there are also sterling schools free of danger or of discipline problems of note and from which students get top grades in nationwide exams. High schools offer a very wide variety of courses and separate the college-bound students from the vocational ones. In many schools, even when the average standard is low, an excellent education is available to those who take advantage. "You could learn an awful lot here if you listened," said a visiting Swedish student of her suburban high school.

However, if you are packing your child off to the local school, you cannot assume that it will be satisfactory. You must investigate, preferably before deciding where to live. Many Americans consider a good local school one of the most important criteria in choosing a neighborhood.

Better schools are generally in better areas, but there are scattered success stories everywhere. Poor neighborhoods in big cities may have so-called "magnet" schools, which emphasize particular studies and attract students from all over the city. Some large cities also have at least one select high school, which requires high grades and test scores for admission. These schools are as high-pressure and prestigious as any private school.

By law, schools must provide an education for all students, even those who cannot function in an ordinary classroom. Consequently there are numerous programs for handicapped, retarded, and "developmentally disabled" children.

Beating the System

Overall, unless you're living in a small, one-school town, the school set-up is complicated. Your address determines your child's school assignment, but often it is possible to change that assignment. Perhaps the only way to learn the ins and outs of your local school system is to talk to other parents. You will probably not find it written down anywhere that School A is a good school and School B a bad one. Or School C may be very good if you can get into the gifted program (a fast-track program) and otherwise you're better off elsewhere. These are the things you'll find out by gossiping in the local Laundromat.

You may also discover that you have a good chance of getting into School E if you come from a certain ethnic group, or that if you are really keen on entering School D, you must line up very early in the morning on a certain day.

133

Or Escaping

You may instead decide to follow many Americans (of all colors) to the suburbs. Nice suburbs have fairly safe, homogeneous schools. Another alternative, one chosen by one in eleven American children, is a private school. (Private schools are ones to which parents pay tuition; public schools are supported by taxes.)

Gaining entrance to the well-known schools is highly competitive. In large cities, there are private schools for every need – from the intellectually advanced to the learning disabled. There are also religious schools and schools adhering to particular educational philosophies. But bear in mind that there are affluent city-dwellers who send their children to public schools merely because they want their children to have the broader social experience of a public school.

Lastly, there are boarding schools, mostly for 9th through 12th grades. Some of the old New England boarding schools have educated generations of families. Happily, in recent years these "snob" schools have made considerable efforts to recruit students from varied backgrounds. Simply being a foreigner may make your child a desirable candidate from the school's point of view.

Private school costs might run from $2,000 a year for a Catholic school (and you don't have to be Catholic to go to one) to $18,000 a year for a boarding school. In my expensive city, annual tuition for private schools averages around $6,000 a year. Nearly all private schools have some scholarships, and the oldest ones have endowments large enough for them to accept anyone they want – regardless of ability to pay.

Universities

Over half of high school graduates go on to some kind of advanced study so there is nothing exclusive about a college education. At last count, there were 3,331 institutions of higher learning in the United States. This includes everything from two-year colleges with a few hundred students to state universities (a university offers both a four-year undergraduate program and advanced degrees from its various graduate schools) with 35,000 students on one campus.

Nearly every college charges tuition. State universities are much cheaper than private ones, where total costs including room and board currently run around $18,000 a year. (It has been noted that the annual cost of a private college education has over the years kept pace with the price of a fully equipped, four-door Chevrolet sedan.) Students from needy families, however, can find scholarships.

Despite the plethora of colleges, every year tension mounts as high school seniors wait to find out if the colleges of their choice have accepted them. The criteria for acceptance include high school grades, personal recommendations, achievements outside school, and test scores. These tests consist of nationwide, though private, exams known as SAT's (Scholastic Aptitude Tests), which test both mathematics and verbal skills, and Achievement Tests, which test knowledge in particular subjects. Although important, these tests do not inspire any of the suicidal impulses that the big exams in other countries do.

A status education is available only from the relatively few high-profile institutions among the many, although an excellent education is actually available at most schools. It is conversely possible to go to one of the "best" schools and emerge with a dim education. The standards for completing the course may not be as demanding as those for entrance, and students often find they have a great deal of time to "party." Some schools are best known for such qualities as the regular drunkenness of their students or the excellent nearby skiing. Admittedly, these are not the elite ones.

Despite such manifestly immature pursuits, in the last fifteen years universities have relinquished their parental role. Most colleges do very little to regulate the lives of students, other than to dismiss those who fail too many courses and to offer counseling to the troubled. Teachers do not involve themselves in the lives of their

135

students. Parents who want supervision for their young might have to find a Christian college.

A Tanzanian who arrived here to attend Corning Community College says he'll never forget the first day's registration: "It was terrible, overwhelming. I had never had to choose my courses before. This would never happen in Africa." American colleges require certain basic courses (varying with each college), but beyond these leave students free to pursue their own interests. Consequently, nearly every institution has a fat catalog with a giant smorgasbord of courses – from Social Relations among the Inuit to nuclear physics.

Graduate Schools

Beyond the parties, remedial courses, and football teams, there is a higher level at which the American university is manifestly successful. It is in the graduate schools that the American academic system comes into full throttle, where intelligent inquiry and the analytic tradition pay off.

The serious student who reaches the advanced levels will be as well trained as at any university in the world. Professors from around the world flock to American universities as much for the intellectual excitement as for the handsome salaries. (Professors are held in much higher esteem than schoolteachers, which is reflected in their salaries as well as in a much greater degree of autonomy in their teaching.) Increasingly, foreigners occupy a large number of places in American graduate schools, particularly in the sciences.

The Classroom

The participatory classroom is the American ideal. Teachers want evidence that the students are interested, listening, and excited. Usually, this comes in the form of questions, and students are sometimes graded on "classroom participation." Foreigners are often surprised that the teacher wants to hear what they think and what they don't understand. Teachers even welcome disagreement.

There is, however, in nearly every class one student who talks too much and bores everybody. You should not become so carried away with the American system that you become this student.

Teachers may want very much for their students to learn, but they do not feel insulted if a student does not understand, or responsible if a student fails. The ultimate effort is up to the student.

The Licensing of America

A century ago, very few occupations required licensing. Doctors, lawyers, and accountants learned their trades through apprenticeships. Today, those who want to go into these reliably lucrative fields need years of postgraduate training. Even many service occupations, such as beautician, electrician, and plumber, have training requirements that restrict membership.

Until World War II, many successful businessmen had little schooling; now most prospective managers need college degrees, and those with an MBA (Master of Business Administration) are most in demand. A degree from one of the prestigious schools commands a high starting salary. Teachers and social workers, besides acquiring a bachelor's degree (conferred on completing the undergraduate course) must submit to specialized training.

This is a trend that James Fallows, one of our more alert social observers, deplores. At its best, he explains in his book, *More Like US*, America was a country with enormous receptivity for anyone who could do the task at hand, regardless of whether or not he had specific credentials. The diploma mill, he is convinced, has done little to improve people's skills. It just serves to keep people in their places – an unhealthy development for this country, keeping people without academic talent or tuition fees from getting ahead. Furthermore, as one only has one youth to spend in preparation, lengthy training greatly restricts people's flexibility. Fallows suggests we change our system to encourage the talented teachers and the gifted doctors, instead of the drones. Until then, he is correct in observing that degrees do matter, and for many fields, it is worth the effort of getting one.

Adult Education

After complaining about many aspects of American life, a 40-year-old woman from Hong Kong concluded, "But where else could someone my age go back to school and get a degree in social work? Here you can change your whole life, start a new business, do what you really want to do."

So at least to this person, school requirements weren't inhibiting. And to millions of others, adult education is the path to a new career, or if not to a new career, to a new outlook. Schools generally encourage the older person who wants to start anew, and besides regular classes, schedule evening classes in special programs. Today there are so many people of retirement age in college that it is no longer remarkable.

Chapter Nine

FRIENDS

There's often a disappointment waiting for the newcomer who takes American friendliness at face value. Americans are indiscriminate with their smiles and their chatter. Foreigners (those who come from places where people don't behave like friends unless they are friends) on arrival may be delighted to find themselves the objects of much enthusiastic attention and imagine they have instantaneously acquired a slew of fine friends. "But it doesn't mean anything," says an Indian woman.

"Often the first American we sit down and talk to is at the employment agency, and she's so nice we think we've got this wonderful new friend. Then we find out it was just for profit, and we never hear from her again. We're disillusioned."

This is not to say that Americans will always let you down. Many foreigners have found Americans to be not only friendly, but loyal and helpful. However, the mobility of American life has made the term "friend" less profound than elsewhere.

In many countries, most friends date from schooldays, and it is hard to make new ones thereafter. For Americans it is the exception rather than the rule to remain in one place, and the school friends are usually left behind. New friends rise up to fill new stages of life. Even when the locale remains the same, new friends step in to match life changes: college friends, work friends, club friends, neighbors, new-hobby friends, sports friends, friends-with-same-age-children.

Frequently, each friend fills a particular niche. There's the friend with whom I discuss certain problems, the one with whom I play tennis, the one with whom I work. When anything changes – my problems go away, I quit tennis, I get a new job – I may stop seeing those particular friends. If I'm lucky, I will have a few lifelong friends, but these could be scattered about the world.

The Rules

Once I've got a friend, I'll be careful not to presume on him/her. That we might be "bothering" someone is an everlasting concern of Americans, even among good friends.

"Irish people live in each other's pockets," said one woman. "It's completely different here. You keep your distance."

I will be very hesitant to ask friends for favors – one of my attractions as a friend is that I am not demanding. If I were, my prospective friends would be likely to back off. Neediness scares people. Rather than having to refuse a request, we prefer to have friends we can trust to make their requests rare and reasonable.

We ourselves do not wish to be indebted to anybody else. We

like reciprocal arrangements because they keep the scales balanced. This week I drive my friend to the airport; next week she drives me. A Chinese woman related that she tried to join a childcare cooperative, but she found the accounting system so complex (to make sure that no one person did more than anyone else) that it drove her crazy.

Eventually in a friendship one can begin to take small services for granted – the loan of a dress, a phone call to find out vital information – but no one expects a real sacrifice. No matter how desperately my friend might need a babysitter, she would never ask me to miss a day's work to take care of her child. I have sometimes been very confused when foreign friends did remarkable things for me – drove me great distances or took the subway to the airport to meet me. Such things are not in our vocabulary, and I find it difficult to respond.

For the average American, the feeling of being indebted is practically a physical pain. When a neighbor had to store some things in my freezer (which was no trouble for me) after hers broke down, she could not rest until she had made me a special dinner. I rescued another neighbor's runaway dog, and she bought me a cake. In point of fact, most of us are human and like to be helpful and would not mind receiving only thanks for a good deed.

It is not a coincidence that the only person on our block who borrows our garden tools was born in Trinidad. We are delighted to loan them, but our other neighbors would rather buy their own, even if it means spending a lot for something they use once a year.

Attitudes are different in small towns where people know each other well. In rural areas most people don't have the money to buy tools they will use once a year, and a great deal of socializing goes on in the name of borrowing and returning things. In the cities, affluence has afforded independence, but it is significant that Americans would rather put their money into independence than into other luxuries.

Best Friends

In the special category of lifelong friends, the favor scorecard is not so carefully kept. But here the potential for favor-giving must be more or less equal. This is one reason it is difficult to have good friends across economic gaps. If you fly me to your villa in Spain, how can I possibly repay you?

Privacy

"In Malaysia, you don't have to hire a caterer," says one friend of mine. "We just mention we're having a party, and everybody comes over to help."

Here, one reason I'm not going to arrive in the morning to help out is that I would be infringing on the party-givers' privacy. They are not obligated to have anyone outside the family in their house until the first guest arrives, and they don't want me looking inside their cupboards and listening to them bicker about how many bottles of wine to buy.

Furthermore, if I insist on helping, I would seem to be suggesting that they are unable to manage alone. Even when I have a very close friend in need, I will go to lengths to appear not to be inconveniencing myself by helping. Part of my kindness to my friend is to act as if I think she can manage perfectly well without me.

Perhaps she is sick. I will make a casserole dish for her and take it to her house, which is some distance away. I may tell her that the dish was something left over after feeding my family (when perhaps in fact I shopped and cooked especially to make it for her) and that I happened to be in her area anyhow (highly unlikely). She may suspect the truth but will appreciate my consideration of her feelings.

Big Trouble

All this delicacy is very tough on people who are really in trouble. Americans are largely protected against catastrophe, but when big trouble strikes – such as a long illness in the family – it can be disillusioning to discover that one's friends are not going to do very much. The troubled family may be desperate enough to accept any amount of help, but their friends scarcely know how to offer and, besides, are not in the habit of sacrificing much time for others.

While some Americans report great help from friends during divorce, a Japanese man told me how terribly isolated he felt when he was going through his divorce here. No support net closed around him as it would have in Japan. American friends wouldn't have wanted to insult him by appearing to think he was needy. Indeed, an American might well feel smothered by too much attention. Even in our sorrow, we like some time to be alone.

Some foreigners have observed that Americans prefer to help in an institutionalized way. In the AIDS crisis, many people have volunteered through agencies to help the sick. The sick person feels more comfortable calling the agency than his friends; his need is legitimized. The volunteer finds the agency route more straight-forward than trying to help a friend who is sick – who would probably endlessly protest, "Oh, please, you've done too much already."

These protests are for the self-esteem of the recipient. You can assume that if someone offers to do something for you, he would genuinely like to do it. Because we don't feel responsible for others, we don't offer anything we don't want to deliver. And if the offer is turned down, we will also take the refusal at face value.

I do not mean to convince readers that they will find no helpful friends. Many people in America do not live by the "rules" outlined here, and the country is full of good souls who exist to be of use to others. For true Christians, giving is supposed to be the heart of their religion so by all means let them practice it.

The Civilities

Most foreigners note that Americans are constantly saying "Please," "Thank you," and "You're welcome."

"It's hypocritical," says a Chinese man, "they don't really mean it." It's true that it doesn't mean much, but it is an acknowledgement that you don't expect people to do things for you. Even when you do – such as when receiving change in a store – you will appear rude if you don't give thanks.

"You're welcome" troubles some newcomers with its insinuation that one has actually done something worth being thanked for. You can always say instead, "Oh, it was nothing," but if it really was nothing, it's best to stick with "You're welcome."

Neighbors

It can come as a disappointment to foreigners to move into an American community and discover neighbors whose neighborliness ends with saying hello. In many countries to be a neighbor presumes a relationship. Here, it can be almost the opposite.

Since early days in America, heterogenous groups have lived side by side, but living side by side didn't mean they liked each other. When a Scotsman staked out his claim on the frontier, he didn't know who would move in next. It could be a German, a Norwegian, a Jew – someone who wasn't his kind. It was true that people needed each other out in the wild, but they were also suspicious of each other.

We remain cautious in approaching our neighbors until we find out what kind of people they are. The neighbor is in a position to be the biggest bother of anyone we know. This is the person who could drop in anytime, comment on our comings and goings, do weird things with our children. One might retort that this is also the person who could most conveniently be helpful to us, but help we're not supposed to need.

One reason people move from small towns to big cities is to get away from nosey neighbors, to live in blissful anonymity. The price, of course, is isolation.

Homogeneous communities are closer. On military compounds

or in university housing you will find groups who reach out readily to the new arrivals in their midst. A factor separating neighbors is that even the inhabitants on a block of identically priced houses may have little in common. A blue-collar worker who spends all weekend watching sports on television may live next door to a poet who spends her spare time weaving. On the other side, you may have computer programmers living in another world entirely.

The design of houses and the privacy of garages also limit neighborliness. It is possible to live next door to someone and simply never meet him. In the suburbs, whereas people used to pause to chat when they arrived home in the evening, now the automatic garage door opener allows them to glide into their garages and disappear with only a wave. Gardens bring neighbors together, but in the long summer evenings people are more likely to be indoors watching *The Golden Girls* on television than working the earth.

As might be expected, there are many lonely people in America. A Brazilian told me that she thinks people watch television so much because they're lonely – "they have no neighbors to talk to."

Moving On

Some neighbors do become fast friends, and you shouldn't assume that you won't. What is likely, though, is that you or your neighbors are going to be moving on at some point, and you will have to start all over again making friends with somebody else. Two out of five Americans move every five years.

A person's feeling of community often does not come from the place he lives. Some people's community is the workplace, or their community is made up of a group of people with similar interests. Household isolation is exacerbated by the increasingly great distances people live from their work. In turn, the community suffers because people spend so much time commuting that they have little time left for community activities.

Meeting and Greeting

INTRODUCTIONS Introductions are casual here and do not signify much (unlike countries where an introduction establishes a relationship). It is more polite to introduce two people than not to, and it places neither under an obligation. If you are with one friend and encounter another, you need only say,

"Ralph Scott, this is Mike Phan."

The more honored party is the one introduced to (in this case, Ralph), but this quaint rule needn't concern you much. Status is of little matter here. Unless there is business at hand, nobody need produce a card (and often not then). When introduced, you only respond with a smile and "Nice to meet you" or "How are you?" (To

A firm grip, a smile, and a direct gaze into the other person's eyes make up a proper handshake.

which the reply is, "Fine, thank you.") If you are seated and the other person is standing, you should rise, unless you are a lady to whom a man is being introduced. Conversation may or may not ensue.

HANDSHAKES People meeting for business and older people greeting each other socially usually shake hands. People who see each other regularly would not ordinarily shake hands. Men shake hands more than women. If two couples are introduced at a party, the men would shake hands and the women may or may not. Because I like the extra cordiality of the handshake, I nearly always shake hands when I meet someone, unless the circumstances are very casual. Shaking hands on leaving a party is entirely optional. No one will think you rude if you don't, but anybody is glad to shake any hand that is offered.

Do grip the other person's hand firmly (but not so firmly as to crush the bones) and give a couple of springy pumps up and down. The passive extending of a hand, leaving someone else to do the work of shaking, leaves a bad impression. People will think you're a) conceited; and b) lazy.

THE SOCIAL KISS One form of greeting widely replaces the handshake – the pseudo-kiss. To execute this, one leans forward from the waist and presses one's cheek against the other person's, simultaneously kissing the air. One hand usually comes up to simulate a hug, except the hand will stop short of the back and grab the shoulder. While appearing to add warmth, this hand may actually be protecting against too much body contact. Or the hand may pat the other person's back, which is an assertion that what is going on has no sexual meaning. The two people will avoid pressing their bodies together. You go through this routine on one cheek only.

This kind of kissing is on the rise among sophisticates and even business acquaintances. It means little. Women and women do it; men and women do it. Men and men do not do it; they stick to shaking hands.

147

Photos: Kristy MacDonald

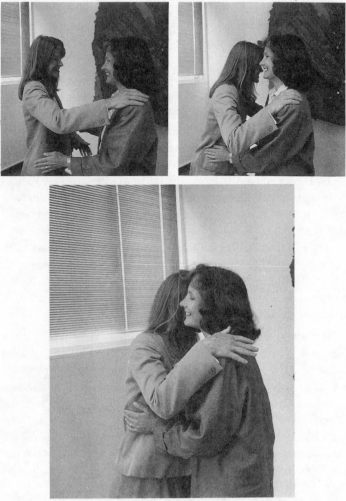

This sequence shows the social kiss as two women greet each other. Note that despite the obvious warmth, the bodily contact is actually quite limited. The kiss itself flies off into the air.

Photo: The Weekly Packet

A high school baseball team celebrating its victory. Sports victories provide acceptable occasions for boys or men to hug each other.

MEN STUFF Backslapping is acceptable among men. So is a touch or a squeeze of the shoulder. But only ball players in their moments of triumph are certifiably masculine enough to throw their arms around each other.

The New Sensitive Male cropped up in the seventies in reaction to the too-macho standoffish man of the last generation. This new breed does a lot of self-conscious hugging, but most men limit bodily same-sex contact to throwing an arm around another's shoulders.

Couples In Love

Public displays of affection between couples, disgusting to some Asians, are acceptable here. Deep soulful kissing in broad daylight is not in the best of taste, but we would not consider it too remarkable either. Handholding, touching, squeezing, and even little kisses are

149

to us just couples properly demonstrating their mutual happiness. Only if a couple is too wrapped up in each other to notice the others present would we consider it rude and make jokes about it later.

When teenagers "can't keep their hands off each other," their parents may not be charmed, but they find some compensation in noting their children's normal sexual adjustment.

Friend or Boyfriend?

Women usually have women friends while men have men friends, but it is perfectly possible for friendships to cross gender lines. Women like to feel that a man's interest in them needn't be sexual. But partly because there is often some confusion about whether it is or isn't, close male-female friendships are in the minority.

Foreign men need to realize that the seeming looseness of American women (or girls) does not mean that they are sexually available. Although many young American women are not virgins, many have no desire to go to bed with someone they do not love, and few wish to have sex with many men.

In some countries, if a woman makes friendly overtures it means she's offering sex. Here, it emphatically does not. A woman may act especially nice because she feels sorry for a poor man alone in a foreign country. When the man misconstrues her kindness as a desire for sex, she is infuriated.

The same is true of skimpily dressed women. Skintight slacks, see-through tops, and bikini bathing suits may clothe a girl who hopes to catch a man's eye, but her style of dress should not be taken to indicate that any man will do or that she combines sex and the profit motive.

What Do I Call You?

It was not so twenty years ago, but first names are now the rule in America. If Ralph meets Mike through Dan, all will immediately call each other by first names. Socially, only in the most formal circles, or when a young person is addressing someone considerably older, need one hesitate before risking the first name.

The first name is the given name. Most babies also get a middle name, which is less used. The last name is the family name and is inherited from the father. Thirty years ago, women universally took their husbands' family names upon marriage, sometimes keeping their former last name as a middle name. A woman might then become Harriet Beecher (her father's name) Stowe (her husband's name). She would be known widely as Mrs. (which denotes a married woman) Stowe, and letters would arrive addressed to Mrs. Calvin Stowe. Her husband would remain forever Mr. Calvin Stowe.

Times have changed, and the women's movement has made many women reluctant to change their names for the sake of a husband. Thus I remain Esther Wanning, although married. I am occasionally called Mrs. Lipsey (my husband's name), but I could not properly be called Mrs. Wanning because that would make me the Mrs. of someone named Wanning, which I am not.

That leaves me with two possible titles: Miss, which is the usual title for an unmarried woman or girl but is proper for married women retaining their own last names (such as Miss Elizabeth Taylor), or else Ms. – pronounced *mizz* – which is the feminist alternative to Mr. and does not denote a marital state. Ms. is widely used in newspapers and on business letters but is less often spoken.

These complications and the fact that so many women have divorced and remarried makes it much easier just to call everyone by first name. This only leaves the problem that using a first name connotes a familiarity that not everybody likes. An older person, in particular, may much prefer that people with whom she does business call her Mrs. Stevens rather than Mary.

Your friend's friends will expect you to use their first names, but if in other situations you have any doubts as to whether a first name is appropriate, start with the more formal address (i.e., Mr. Smith) and wait for the other party to insist that you call him Fred. If somebody calls you by your first name, then you are free to use his or hers (unless you are very young or talking to a doctor who is nearly always called "Dr."). Even children regularly call adults by first name, to the dismay of many. Teachers, however, should be addressed formally, unless they insist otherwise.

In offices nearly everybody is now on a first-name basis, including the Chief Executive Officer. But if instant familiarity makes you uncomfortable, stick to your own way. I am charmed to be called Miss Wanning.

Nicknames

Some people are universally known by their nicknames, which may or may not relate to their actual first names. Many are holdovers from childhood. Such names as Tinky, Buzz, Butch, and Muffie are rarely on a birth certificate. A Robert is often called Bob, a William called Bill, and a Richard called Dick. A John is called Jack, a James, Jim. Other names are simple diminutives – Mike from Michael; Dan from Daniel; Liz from Elizabeth; Art from Arthur. Then there's Hal from Harold; Steve from Stephen; Sally from Sarah.

However, many Roberts are called Robert, etc. You may need to ask, "Do you go by Robert or Bob?"

The latest crop of children seem to be known by nicknames much less than former generations. Presumably this is because there are fewer of them and so each one has assumed an importance too great to be reduced to a nickname. An Alexander in his crib is called Alexander; a little Benjamin is no longer known as Benny; Katherines aren't Kathy. This may also be because people are more inclined now to choose a favorite name, rather than name the child after a revered relative. So little Benjamin is not going to be confused with Uncle Benjamin, nor does he need to fill his shoes.

Conversation

It is hard to generalize about conversation in America. We have the full range of talkers – chatty, taciturn, forthcoming, secretive. Conversation is generally less lively than in the Latin countries, where everyone talks at once. When someone talks here, everyone is expected to listen, no matter how dull the talker may be. But there are countries where the conversation is far more careful and deliberate than ours.

In the search for conversational material, work is a good bet. In many countries, it is not seemly to ask, "What do you do?" Not so here. We are so often defined by our work that we are happy to talk about it. But if work proves unproductive, you might try, "What do you do in your spare time?"

We are not on the whole a reticent people. Some observers have noted that we are freer than Asians in discussing emotions and feelings, but more secretive about factual matters. You can safely inquire about wives or husbands, children, geographical background, hobbies, and habits. Ethnicity is a subject of some interest, and Americans will inquire about the ancestry of others.

A highly personal conversation can take place on the basis of short acquaintance, but it will not indicate that a lasting friendship has been established. Americans can form relationships very quickly, but they don't often go deep. We constantly encounter new people we will never see again. Therefore we don't need to worry that our familiarity will entice them to become burdens to us. Airplanes are famous for inducing intimate conversations, doubtless because no follow-up is expected.

While few Americans will mind any questions you may ask – particularly if they are in the spirit of intercultural research – you may find they are delicate about asking you questions. One Chinese friend of mine says, "Americans aren't interested in other people. They don't ask questions."

My other Chinese friend says, "Ah, that's not true. They just find things out in a more roundabout manner."

We worry about invading people's privacy, and we also have the idea that foreigners aren't used to personal inquiries. So some Americans may chatter on about trivialities because they don't dare to plunge into deeper territory, but given an opening will happily take your lead. Others will resolutely talk about safe and superficial subjects until the cows come home. And still others have much to say on important but impersonal subjects, which interest them more than personal ones. (This distribution is probably not unlike the differences anywhere.)

What we have very little of are pre-cut conversational rites. Even when engaging in small talk, you have to make up your own lines.

Safe and Unsafe Subjects

You won't find Americans quick to take up the subject of religion, which is considered a personal matter. As a newcomer to the country, you could certainly ask about religious habits, but Americans who meet at parties do not inquire about each other's practices.

Politics are discussed among people who are in relative agreement, but when a group is far apart, politics becomes a subject to be avoided. On the whole, we dislike argument. Unlike the French, who consider a verbal battle refreshing, we become personally insulted by disagreement. If an argument breaks out, we try to smooth it over or break it up.

The best way to do so is to return to the harmless topics. Many of these are questions of taste. Did you like such-and-such a movie? What do you think of the food at that new restaurant? Do you like Mexico? How do you like the weather? Through discussing mutual likes and dislikes, we find out whether this is our kind of person. American society is classed by tastes as much as by anything else.

Compliments are always in order. "What a pretty dress ... I love your earrings … What a nice tie." (But not, "How much did you pay?") We keep the compliments flowing even with close friends and family. The recipient should accept the compliment graciously by looking very pleased and saying, "Oh, thank you." The tale of the item in question often provides further talk.

Most of the people you meet will be glad to hear about your country and about your impressions of America. You can be frank. We've become accustomed to criticism in recent years, although of course it's always tactful to mix a few positive comments in with the negative. ("The bus stations are awful, and I hate the food, but the people are friendly.")

There are two subjects that may rapidly bring conversation to a halt: age and money. Only as a newcomer might you plead innocent of these sanctions. If you insist on asking someone's age, it's best to lower your voice, inquire "Do you mind if I ask your age," then immediately respond with "Heavens! You look much younger!" All adult Americans are mad to look young. Actually, many of them do.

Income is a very hush-hush subject, and while we may spend a great deal of time wondering how much other people make, we don't say so. This may be because, all evidence to the contrary, we hold to the idea that people are actually paid according to their worth, and we don't care to have that figure public knowledge.

We do not inquire about how much people paid for things either, unless we have a good reason to do so. ("I'm shopping for a new car myself. Could you tell me what that one cost you?") People who have got a great bargain are glad to volunteer the cost, but they hate to be caught overpaying.

You also should not poke too obviously into someone's class background. You do not ask, "What did your father do for a living?" To ask where someone went to college, you need a cue. ("Ah, you rowed on the Charles River; did you go to Harvard?")

Sex is, as in many cultures, best approached with discretion. Most direct questions are taboo, and probably people will grow uncomfortable if you are overly frank in presenting your own history. All appearances to the contrary, we don't take sexual matters for granted. I write, however, from a woman's point of view. I understand that men may among themselves make up great tales of conquest. Women usually discuss methods of birth control only with close friends.

You do not inquire into someone's sexual orientation. "Are you gay?" is a forbidden question.

When all other conversation fails, there are always sports and the children to fall back on. If you are male, an interest in the fortunes of the local football and baseball team may serve you well at parties.

Bluntness and Tact

Americans can be very direct, which may be discomfiting to people from more circuitous cultures. Here, if your neighbor thinks your apple tree is encroaching on his garden, he will tell you, rather than hint at the subject. If you claim New York is the capital of the United States, you will quickly learn you're wrong (it's Washington, D.C.). A supervisor who thinks you're making too many mistakes will let you know.

The bluntness is somewhat tempered by language. Besides a profusion of Please's and Thank You's, a well-spoken person will make his points politely. "Would you mind if I borrowed your atlas?" not "Lend me your atlas." "Perhaps you could be more careful," says the supervisor to the blunderer. "I think you're a bit off there," to the person who added two and two and got five. The meaning is still clear, but a little delicacy of language leaves some respect for the other person's feelings. "I don't think you're quite right about that," goes down better than "No, you're wrong."

Criticism

Friends do not often directly criticize each other, and people who do not "mind their own business" are disdained. Even parents aghast at their grown children's behavior may choose to say nothing rather than alienate their offspring. "They have to live their own lives and make their own mistakes," say the parents with a sigh. Popular psychology insists that people's behavior comes from deep, unconscious motivations, and people can't change until they understand why they act the way they do. So, according to this theory, only a professional therapist can help them. You, their friend, would only make them angry and unhappy by offering unwanted advice.

Style of Talk

Americans admire someone who thinks fast and always has something to say. Among friends, there's apt to be a lot of cheerful banter going on. This very volubility makes some cultures distrust Americans and consider them insincere. If someone has something to say about everything, how much could she really know?

On the other hand, there are those – the French, for instance – who find Americans ponderous talkers. Ask a question, and you'll get a long-winded answer. Talk isn't lighthearted exchange for us; it's informational exchange, and we assume you want all the data you can get. In some cultures, people will take the opinion of a trusted friend. Not us. We want the facts so that we can make up our own minds. As nearly every cultural observer has noted, Americans love statistics.

What we do not like is silence. Should everyone in a group run out of things to say, an anxious pall descends until somebody saves the day by producing a subject. For the party teetering on the brink of silence (which quite a few are), almost any subject will do. By no means are all Americans slick talkers. Some of the younger ones in particular, having spent their formative years sitting silently before the television, do not seem to have developed much verbal ability. These are not, however, the cream of our crop and will be sadly handicapped, whatever field they enter.

Talking About Me

Compared to some peoples, we can be very boastful, and we see nothing wrong with stating our credentials frankly. However, smart conversationalists keep an edge of self-deprecation in their comments: "The company chose me to go to China so they'd have some peace in the office for a while."

Or: "That was a lucky shot. I'm really a terrible golfer." You are, incidentally, not supposed to agree.

Gestures

Many Americans, eager to be understood, will use all possible means of communication, including lively gesturing with the hands and arms. The hands are intended to add emphasis and conviction, but only rarely are they lifted higher than the shoulders. Other Americans, often of Anglo-Saxon origin, do not consider gesticulation dignified and are, in fact, somewhat wooden in their movements.

Gestures are anything but universal, sometimes bearing opposite meanings in different cultures, so the language of gestures is an important one to learn. Several of our most well-meaning signals are obscene in other countries.

Headshaking. Up and down is yes, and from left to right is no.

Waving. The arm is held upward, palm outward, fingers stretched out. The hand moves from side to side in a V pattern. Can mean hello or goodbye.

Snapping fingers. An attention-getting motion, not gracious, but not vulgar. May also mean, "I just remembered something."

Arms folded across chest. Not rude or arrogant but could mean, "I'm waiting."

Bowing. We don't do it.

Striking forehead. Somebody who strikes her own forehead with an open palm is saying, "How stupid I am."

Pointing to own chest. "Do you mean me?"

Hitchhiking. Hold arm away from body, make a fist, then extend thumb. Not a vulgar gesture, as in some parts of the world.

Come here. Hold arm forward, make a fist, palm up. Extend thumb and forefinger and wiggle forefinger.

Hand wag. Fingers out and palm down. "It was so-so." Indicates lukewarm response to something.

Finger Signs

Thumb to nose. Very rude. Shows defiance.

Crossed fingers. "Good luck" or "Hope for the best." Among children, there is a code that a lie is not a lie if the fingers are crossed.

Pointing with forefinger stuck upwards. "Look that way."

V-sign. Either "We have won," or "We will win." Also, "Peace." Palm can face forwards or backwards.

Thumb pointed up. Success.

Thumb pointed down. Failure.

One or both index fingers pointed upwards from fist. "We're number one." Used mainly at sporting events.

Middle finger stuck up from fist. An obscene gesture of contempt.

Circle out of thumb and forefinger, other fingers sticking up. "Okay." "It's a go."

Telephoning

The telephone call has replaced the social call in this country. While dropping in on people uninvited is often a bad bet, you can drop in on them nearly anytime via telephone. You do not, however, wish to wake up the person you're calling. If you have no idea what sort of hours somebody keeps, you should probably try not to call after 9 p.m. in the evening or before 8 a.m. in the mornings (later on weekends).

It's nice to inquire "Are you busy?" when you call. Even if you don't, callees are expected to decline to chat if the phone has rung at an inconvenient moment. They need only offer to call back. A large portion of the population now has answering machines, and you should not hesitate to leave a message, being sure to leave your own number spoken clearly and slowly. If you receive messages, you should try to return calls within 24 hours. If you receive a phone call while you have company, you should not chat but should offer to call back at a mutually convenient time. This remains the case even if the call is long distance.

Many foreigners could afford to work on the way they say "hello" when they answer the phone. You will notice that Americans often have a pleasant, anticipatory note (the last syllable drawn out and rising in tone) in their voices, as if they're already implying "How nice to hear from you." A dead, flat tone as in "What bill collector is bothering me now?" does not endear the caller.

Most telephone calls have some purpose. Only with very close friends do I feel free to call merely because I'm lonely or have something on my mind. However, I can often think of some reason ("I wondered if you knew of a good sushi restaurant?") to lift up the phone if I'm in the mood. Whereupon, a very long and pleasant conversation may ensue, having little to do with sushi.

Chapter Ten

SOCIAL LIFE

ENTERTAINING

Some Americans carry on immensely busy social lives, and others live in virtual isolation. Some spend most of their time with their families, and others see almost everybody except their families. Some people love parties, and some hate them.

Social class is a determinant here. The upper classes, having more time and money at their disposal than most, entertain and visit a great deal. The lower classes, less mobile and lacking space for large parties, are more apt to limit their social lives to church suppers and their families.

It's the middle classes (which means most Americans) that get headaches over entertaining. It's for them that magazines run endless articles about party food, serving, decorating, and manners. The articles serve only to fuel middle-class American anxiety over being hosts and hostesses.

We have the impression that the good life involves lots of gay parties. The affluence of America has given large numbers of people the leisure, money, and space to invite people to their homes merely in order to pass the time. But it doesn't come naturally to many of us. Entertaining, besides being a lot of work, is stressful.

The magazines have convinced us that "an informal dinner" requires very out-of-the-ordinary preparations – elegant foods, special wines, flower arrangements, a clean house. This is a lot of work – if you have no servants – just in order to sit around and talk.

Some people love to cook, but many are acutely aware that they have nothing in their repertoires that will do for parties. We are at a disadvantage because the dishes we were brought up on (roast beef, fried chicken) are neither healthy nor gourmet. So we must pore over cookbooks making up the menu, shop at specialty markets, and arduously follow the small print of the recipes. Lining up the guests can be a challenge too as many people have their Saturday evenings, the most usual night for a dinner party, scheduled weeks in advance.

The truth is many Americans really don't enjoy this form of socializing. It's set, strained, difficult – and most of our friends are not such brilliant conversationalists that it seems worth the bother.

Why a Party?

Nonetheless, entertain we must. It's a requirement of middle-class life, and people who don't fulfill it feel guilty and are constantly muttering, "We must have the so-and-so's over." A party may be given in celebration of an occasion (birthday, wedding, graduation) or to honor a visitor, but more commonly takes place for no other reason than "the fun of it."

164

Two decades ago, company wives were expected to entertain in order to boost their husbands' careers; now that many wives are more interested in their own careers, the business dinner is likely to take place in a restaurant. Business gatherings have an advantage in that people are doing what they really like best: working. But aside from business, there are still any number of reasons for throwing a party.

If nothing else, one wants to show off the house. Many Americans are obsessed with home decorating and after having spent a large amount of time and money in fixing up the place, it's nice to have people come and admire the results (do try to find something nice to say about people's homes when you visit). After all, we discourage people from dropping in (partly because we don't like to be caught with a messy house) so what is the large living room for?

Another motivation for having parties is that our families are often either physically far apart or spiritually distant. A gathering of friends is an attempt to fill the empty place left by the dispersal of the clan. No one wants to feel alone in the universe. We may not want friends to take up too much of our time, but we do want to have them. It's one measure of success, and parties are an efficient way to keep in touch with scattered acquaintances. And of course, party obligations and social debts must be returned if one wishes to continue to have a social life.

The Guests

Visitors from afar may be surprised at how homogeneous the guests are at a party – no old mothers or dotty uncles or polite children. People tend to socialize with their own age groups. Children have children's parties; old people have old people's parties. If you find otherwise, you have probably happened in on a family party, or have arrived in rural circles.

This homogeneity of age, however, does not necessarily assist the conversational flow. Because Americans move around and change jobs so much, many of them do not belong to any particular social circle, and their various friends often do not know each other. In fact, the hosts themselves sometimes barely know their guests. They round up their disparate acquaintances in the optimistic hope that some party magic will take over and make the fun.

Too often, conversation falls flat or becomes hard work. We have all at one time or another found ourselves in a room full of strangers looking desperately for a friendly face to talk to. Few hosts find time to do a proper job of introducing people to each other. Under such circumstances, don't hesitate to bluntly introduce yourself. "Hello, I'm Lakshmi Karna," followed by "How do you know the so-and-so's?" are acceptable opening lines from which further conversation can usually be developed.

Other parties consist entirely of the troops from the office. On these occasions too a pall of discomfort can fall, resulting from the general sense that it's inappropriate to discuss business at a party, but unnatural to discuss the weather and such with people one sees every day. In the end, business usually wins out, and then everybody relaxes.

Although such office parties take place, it is not considered necessary to entertain work colleagues. People who are inseparable in the office may have never been to each other's homes. An Indian confided, "When I first came here, I was terribly offended that the people I met at work didn't invite me home. Later, I was glad because I wanted to have time to myself too." For better or worse, our busy lives tend to be compartmentalized.

Once you've accepted an invitation to a party, you must attend. If something happens to prevent you, telephone with your excuses as soon as possible. People work hard to give a party; you must remember that it's nearly always your hosts, not the servants, who have spent the day cooking and cleaning, and they could be very upset if you don't show up. Furthermore, other guests may have been invited specifically to meet you.

Having Fun?

A Chinese man says that what strikes him about American parties is that people rarely seem to be having an awfully good time. I think this is a fair observation. There's a lot of onus involved in being an American – that is, in being individually responsible for one's fate – and it doesn't fly away at a party. We don't arrive surrounded by a family or a culture that makes us feel secure, and the party itself may seem like another test – new people to meet and impress. Some people use alcohol to remove their inhibitions, but many prefer to cope without both the high spirits and the hangover. My Irish friend thinks that American parties are simply too civilized. This is not to say that all American parties are grim. Most are quite pleasant, and some are positively jubilant.

Actually, despite any generalizations I may make, there's a large element of surprise in an American party. The old rules for entertaining have been thrown out, and new ones haven't replaced them. Americans may be as bemused as you are at the form the evening takes. Will the hosts be wearing dress suits or ragged jeans? Will the meal be served as soon as one walks in the door or hours later? Will loud music substitute for conversation? Will the other guests be fascinating and friendly or otherwise? Who knows? Perhaps the hosts will arrive home with the bags of groceries while you're standing on the doorstep. Visitors from abroad, at least, can chalk it all up to cultural experience.

Some people have just given up on the whole effort and meet friends at restaurants. This is an acceptable option.

The Dinner Party

The invitation will probably come by telephone. You needn't say yes or no on the spot ("I'll have to check with my husband and make sure we're free" is standard), but you should provide an answer as soon as possible. If you are married, you can assume that your spouse is invited; unless specified, your children are not. If you are living with a "significant other," that person is usually invited, but it's up to you to make sure that your host knows that the person exists. What you should not do is show up with an unexpected guest – no matter how informal the occasion.

The dress code for a dinner party can be unpredictable, and it's not only foreigners who are puzzled by the dress code. The problem is that there are very few conventions remaining.

People who wear a white shirt and tie to work every day may greet you at the door in jeans. However, if the party includes business associates, a suit is more apt to be in order. Among good friends there's less dressing up, and at a middle-class get-together, you are likely to find gentlemen without ties but wearing good-looking sweaters and slacks. A lot of party dressing consists of looking as if you made an effort for your hosts' sake without forsaking the casual look altogether. Older people, however, may put on suits and dresses to go to their friends' houses.

Women often dress up much more than men – perhaps because there are few opportunities left to wear a pretty dress. At any rate, a woman can always wear dressy pants with a blouse and fit in anywhere. In America, a skirt is more elegant, and more formal, than pants. If you are suffering any doubts as to what to wear, simply ask your hosts ("Is it dressy?").

Protocol

You don't need to walk in the door on the dot of the time you were invited for, but you should arrive within 10 to 20 minutes afterwards. If you're much later, your hosts may grow anxious. American dinner food is usually ready at a particular time and gets overcooked or cold with waiting. At some houses, though, it doesn't matter when you arrive because a protracted cocktail hour will precede dinner. However, as one rarely knows which houses these are, if you are going to be more than half an hour late you should telephone and say so. Whatever you do, don't arrive early.

The old etiquette was to serve dinner 45 minutes after the time of the invitation, and this is still a good rule of thumb. It is customary to offer people a drink as soon as they arrive. "What'll you have to drink?" says the host. "What have you got?" is the usual answer. There is no need for the hosts to provide everything anyone might want. They may reasonably offer only wine, beer, and soft drinks. Some people put out elaborate hors d'oeuvres (appetizers) while others prefer that their guests save their appetites for dinner.

At Table

If the dinner is the least bit formal, guests will be ushered to a dining table to eat. They should hesitate before grabbing seats and ask the hostess where she would like them to sit. If she is a very clever hostess she will have calculated places in advance, probably putting men between women. There is also a fading custom that the place of honor for a man is on the hostess's right and that of a woman on the host's right. Your hosts may say, "Oh, sit anywhere," in which case you may be able to manipulate yourself into a seat next to someone you think you would like to talk to. At any rate, men should not all huddle at one end of the table, leaving the women at the other end.

Don't start eating until everyone has been served. A few families say grace before meals, which is a thank you to God for the food (such as: "Lord, we ask you to bless this food to our use and ourselves to thy service. Amen.") It is embarrassing to be caught with your spoon in your mouth when grace is being said and your head should be bowed. It is nice to repeat "Amen" at the end of the grace.

You may or may not have soup to start, followed by a main course (fish, meat, or perhaps pasta or a casserole) with vegetables. Salad may come before, with, or after the main course. A fattening dessert and coffee generally ends the meal. (See "Table Manners" on pages 95–9 for details on using the silverware).

Asians sometimes go away hungry from American tables because they consider it polite to refuse food when it is first offered. Here, if you say you do not want more, your hosts will believe you and probably will not urge you further. When hosts offer more food, they like their guests to immediately say, "Yes, please. It's delicious." They also like guests who eat everything on their plates. If you fail to, you should explain that good as the food is, you are too full to finish.

Dinner party conversation is often punctuated with exclamations about how delicious the food is. We do not take for granted that someone can cook and tend to rhapsodize whether they do it very well or not. The rest of the conversation may be wide-ranging. It's important to keep it going, and your efforts will be appreciated. Nothing is worse than a dinner at which the party eats in grim silence. Be sure to address your remarks equally to the men and women at the table. Women are as educated and well-read as men and resent not being considered equal conversationalists.

Departing

You should not leave immediately after dinner; doing so would suggest that you could hardly wait to leave. You must let a certain conversational period elapse, and then you should make excuses for going at all. You may, for instance, suddenly look at your watch and say, "Good heavens, look at the time. We really must leave." Or, "Whew, past my bedtime. Early game of golf tomorrow." You should do this before your hosts begin to yawn visibly and look threateningly at you. Staying too late is almost as bad as leaving too early. Your hosts still have the dishes to do. If you are not out by 11 p.m., they probably have cause for complaint, and many parties break up earlier. Should your hosts object vigorously when you start to leave and beg you to stay longer, do – but only if you want to. Before departing, say good-night to the other guests, expressing your pleasure at having seen or met them.

It is excellent manners to telephone the next day and offer

Photo: Esther Wanning

Three generations of a family gather for cocktails at their summer home.

further thanks for the fine time you had, but not everybody does. If you prefer, a note of thanks (even a postcard) is just as good as a phone call – or even better as it takes very little of your time and none of the host's.

Some people may enjoy your company enough to ask you repeatedly to dinner without a return move on your part, but usually you are expected to return the hospitality before being invited back again. This is a convenient custom because if you are not anxious to continue the relationship, you can simply fail to reciprocate. However, if you want to reciprocate in some other way, you can send flowers, or invite your friends to a restaurant or to the theater.

Cocktail Parties
This drinking institution was lagging in popularity a short time ago but is now making a comeback. The cocktail party does have a solid contribution to make to social life as it allows the hosts to entertain a large number of people in a small amount of time. It's largely a

171

stand-up institution so you can invite as many people as you can pack vertically into your house. Very often an invitation will give both start and finish times, for instance 5–7 p.m. In reality, unless the hosts are rushing off to the theater, a 5–7 party would probably go on until at least 8, but guests should arrive by 6:30 anyhow. Cocktail parties are apt to be a bit dressier than other kinds of parties, perhaps because they've survived mainly in old-fashioned circles.

Some cocktail parties will offer only a few potato chips and olives to eat. Others have lavish, delectable displays that suffice nicely for a whole dinner. At a buffet table, you help yourself without waiting for an invitation from your hosts.

There's less emphasis on fancy cocktails now than there used to be since Americans are demonstrably drinking less than formerly. Nonetheless, if you are giving such a party, you should have on hand hard liquor (unless you have religious or moral objections to alcohol in which case you might better give a tea party) – gin, bourbon, scotch, and vodka along with the so-called set-ups (tonic, soda, lime, and plenty of ice). You may in fact discover that most of your guests prefer wine, beer, juice, or plain soda water. A hot, non-alcoholic punch I once made was surprisingly popular.

You should know that if someone drinks too much at your house and has a car accident on the way home, you could be held responsible. If any of your guests do get drunk (and it should certainly not be because you forced drinks upon them), do not allow them to drive. Either keep them with you, drive them home yourself, get someone else to drive them home, or send for a taxi.

The Potluck

This bring-your-own-dish party has taken hold in recent years. Its origins lie in the church social, when a large group would gather for an informal supper, each family bringing a dish. Potlucks have now moved into mainstream society, and you may be invited to bring your share of the victuals to everything from a brunch to a wedding. Such a gathering is usually extremely informal, and you needn't be as precise about whether or not you're attending as for a dinner party (unless it is a wedding).

Some potlucks are so casual that the invitation – often a photocopied sheet sent to practically everyone the party-giver knows – does not even require a reply. But usually there's an RSVP (which is French for "answer please"), and whenever you see RSVP you should reply as soon as possible. You may be instructed in the kind of dish to bring, but if not it is polite – though not obligatory – to ask. It is also helpful if you announce beforehand what you plan to bring. Some people arrive with just a bottle or two of wine, but obviously it would not be a good thing if everybody did that.

The drawback of potlucks, besides having to bring a dish that nobody may eat, is their unpredictability. Most have far too much food (your dish need only be large enough for one course for four people – or the equivalent of one person eating four courses), but I've been to a few where the table was practically bare or the choice was limited to varieties of pasta salad. Some potlucks, however, garner a wonderful array of delectable dishes.

A potluck is much looser in terms of arrival and departure time than the dinner party. Usually eating goes on throughout the party so your dish may be consumed even if you arrive late. It's good to bring something relatively simple from the eating point of view. You can count on plates and forks being available, but if you're bringing soup you'd better bring the bowls too. The casualness of potlucks extends also to dress. It's a rare potluck that requires a suit.

Some foreigners are appalled by the very idea of potlucks. "What's the point?" asks a Chinese man. "To invite people to dinner and to tell them to bring the food?" Potlucks are more often than not thrown by people who are genuinely sociable, but who don't want to spend days cooking for a large crowd. They would say that eating isn't the point of a party anyhow, it's the company.

The Brunch

Brunch is a Sunday morning affair that combines breakfast and lunch, held anywhere between 10 a.m. and 2 p.m. The repast imitates breakfast, usually featuring juice, fruit salad, rolls, and eggs, but anything is possible. Champagne or Bloody Marys (tomato juice and vodka) are often on the menu.

Dress is usually casual/pretty. It is Sunday morning (churchgoing time) so you want to look nice. But degree of dressiness depends on the place and the hosts. An attractive jogging suit could be the thing.

The After-Dinner Party

This is apt to be an anything-goes party. Dress up or dress down, come early or late. The party probably won't be in full swing until quite late in the evening. Loud music may inspire dancing. There will certainly be drinks; food may be scarce or it may be abundant. Try to find your hosts to thank before going home.

Birthday Parties

An adult birthday, unless it's one of some significance, such as 21, 40, 50 or 75, is usually just an excuse for having a party and doesn't need special recognition. You could bring a little present, but there's no need to.

For a children's birthday, however, you must come armed with a present. The price category is tricky. A bag of balloons would look cheap next to other presents, but a remote control car would be far too extravagant. Parents have an unspoken agreement not to go broke on kids' birthday presents and look with disfavor at those parents who overspend. Fortunately, children don't love presents according to their price tags.

Where parents often try to outdo each other is in laying on the entertainment for junior's party. There are those who hire clowns and ponies and caterers and magicians or else sweep the children away to fancy clubs, theater matinees, etc. While this is all very nice (if ostentatious), children remain extremely happy playing the traditional party games – pin-the-tail-on-the-donkey, spider's web, blind man's bluff, musical chairs, etc. – followed by ice cream and cake. The Latin influence from south of the border has brought the piñata to North America; any games you can introduce from your culture will add a memorable note. In fact, if you give your child a birthday party just like the one you would give back home, it will doubtless be a hit. If you're intent on the American kind, card stores or big drugstores often sell booklets that tell how to run a traditional children's birthday party.

RECREATION

Going out to movies and restaurants are central pastimes for many. Now that so many people own video cassette recorders (VCR's), watching movies at home is also a frequent entertainment. But probably nobody's time is as fully occupied as that of the true sports fan.

Spectator Sports

Many American men are deeply involved with sports. This does not necessarily mean that they get any exercise. What they do is watch national teams on television. There are men who follow baseball, football, basketball, hockey, golf, and tennis – which means that for the better part of any weekend they can be found in front of the television set. If they are sociable, their buddies may be watching with them. There are plenty of female sports fans too, but not many women feel as free as men to give up their weekends to watching.

Baseball is the great American unifier and has followers in all income and ethnic groups. Nearly every major city has a team, and as each team plays 162 games a year, following baseball can be time-consuming. The season occupies spring and summer and culminates in the fall World Series, during which the two leading teams play each other. The first to win four games wins the Series.

Photo: Esther Wanning

Ecstatic fans watching their home team win football's annual Super Bowl.

Although called the "World" Series, Canada is the only other country to participate.

Football, played in fall and winter, also has a powerful hold on the country. It should not be confused with the game called "football" elsewhere, which we call "soccer." There is very little kicking in our football, which has more to do with running with the ball and knocking people down. Serious injuries are common in football. Each team only plays 16 games during the regular season, and these take place on Sundays and Monday evenings.

Super-Bowl Sunday, the final football playoff in January, finds half the country glued to the television set, although if the local team is not in the finals, the passion is muted. Friends gather together in front of the largest television in the crowd. Quantities of beer are swilled, and platefuls of food passed around. The food is of the easily eaten variety – hot dogs, potato chips, cold cuts, bread, salads – so that people can fix, eat, and watch simultaneously.

Professional teams, which include basketball and ice hockey teams, are expected to be profitable for their owners, and they

176

certainly are for the television networks. The games allow plenty of time for commercials.

Soccer is of growing importance among schoolchildren in America, but does not exist on the national level. Among adults, most of the soccer playing is done by immigrants, who play passionately but without major financial support. People who want to follow world soccer are good candidates to buy satellite dishes, huge circular antennas that pick up broadcasts from all over the world.

College sports occupy the television screens when nothing else does. Christmas and New Year's Day are devoted to college football. The big universities, which avidly recruit promising players from high schools, are invariably the winners. Whether college players should be intellectually capable is an on-going debate in the sports world. Many colleges feel that if they want their alumni to donate generously to their old school, they need a winning football team. Curiously enough, this seems to be true.

Some adults continue to play baseball after high school and college on amateur teams sponsored by cities, towns, and companies. Although these games are supposed to be purely for fun, foreigners may be surprised at how seriously they are taken. Americans care a great deal about winning.

Active Sports

Not every American man hunts and fishes, but many more do than in the world at large. We have some wild country and clear streams left, and our frontier days, when hunting and eating were intimately entwined, were not so long ago. There are still rural families who count on bagging their annual deer to get through the winter. Most current hunting, however, is for the sport – the opportunity to be outdoors stalking living things through swamp, bush, stream, or woods.

177

Going fishing with the fellows represents heaven to many American males.

Fishing is popular with a large cross-section of the population, and unlike in England, "shooting" is not a particularly upper-class pursuit. The elite may ride to the hounds, but families with racks of rifles over the fireplace are not usually the heirs to old money.

The rich have often rechanneled their killing instincts and are satisfied to go out with their tennis rackets and golf clubs to exclusive country clubs. Tennis and golf, however, are by no means restricted to the monied classes. Public golf courses and tennis courts allow anyone to play, cheaply or for free.

Sailing, motorboating, windsurfing, hang gliding, skiing, kayaking, snowmobiling, mountain climbing, waterskiing, and hiking are a few other avocations that allow Americans to exert themselves outdoors. Many people feel the need to have the best and newest equipment for each sport.

Fitness

The majority of exercise time now is probably logged by people who aren't so much engaged in sports as in keeping fit. People who are keeping fit do not necessarily enjoy the exercise itself, but are looking forward to the sense of well-being that comes afterwards.

High Culture

"What struck me most about the United States when I first came was sex and money," said a Japanese man. He meant by that the importance assigned to both – the bombardment of sexual imagery in advertising and the lust for money.

In the midst of this unrefined landscape, you would not expect much high culture, but in fact the USA shines in many of the arts. There is, however, a great gulf between high culture (classical music, ballet, opera, museum art) and mass culture (movies, television, popular music, hotel art). A small proportion of the public support the museums, opera houses, symphonies, chamber groups, and dance companies.

Nonetheless, the arts are thriving and the caliber of performances high. Most of the financial backing comes from private individuals and foundations, rather than from the government. The classic means of rising in society has been through contributions to the arts, and America has had plenty of rising rich people. In the past decade, many of the Western and Southern cities, which were long considered cultural wastelands, have developed top-flight artistic programs. Recent immigrants contribute greatly to the pool of talent.

HOLIDAYS

Each holiday has its own particular flavor, but most of them only arouse excitement insofar as they provide an excuse for a holiday from work or school. Only Christmas and Thanksgiving inspire great expectations.

179

The Major Holidays

CHRISTMAS "Tis the season to be jolly," says the Christmas song. December 25 celebrates the birth of Christ and is by far the biggest holiday of the year. Its manifestations go far beyond that of its religious origins, and most of the festivities have little to do with religion. In fact, the celebration may originally have been a pagan celebration of the winter solstice (December 21), when the days start to get longer again.

It's Christmas that calls people home from far away to be with their families, and each family has its own Christmas rituals. Although Jews and members of some other religions may prefer not to, most houses have a decorated Christmas tree, and people cook (or buy) special foods for the season – Christmas cookies, plum puddings, fruitcakes. Everybody is expected to have a family or family substitute at Christmas time; it is the only time of year that some families see each other. It is also a particularly depressing time of year for those who are alone.

The central ritual of Christmas is the exchanging of gifts which are intended to represent the "Goodwill towards men" that Christ preached. (See "Gifts" on page 194 for details.) Every year, voices rise to protest the mad commercialism of Christmas, but nothing has dimmed the enthusiasm for gift-giving. As a nation of shameless consumers a holiday centered around shopping suits us very well.

Charitable giving is at a peak at Christmas as well. "Blessed are the poor," said Christ, and so it's a time of year when many people feel inclined to brighten the lives of the less fortunate. An abundance of fine dinners are offered to the poor and homeless on Christmas; the charitable institutions try to emphasize that the need goes on all year.

CHRISTMAS MERRYMAKING A fair proportion of the year's parties are given at Christmastime. As Christmas takes place the week before the new year begins, the holiday spirit does not diminish

Santa Claus is seen everywhere at Christmastime. Little children are told that on the night before Christmas while they are asleep, he comes down the chimney with presents for good children.

even after Christmas. Christmas parties can be given anytime between December 12 and December 29. "Open Houses" are popular, some given on Christmas Eve or Christmas Day.

Family traditions vary. Some people open their presents on Christmas Eve, and some wait until Christmas Day. There are many church services on Christmas Eve; Midnight Mass is popular (usually held at 11 p.m.). Throughout the Christmas season there is much singing of Christmas carols, lovely songs well-known to most Americans. Special concerts play Christmas music, and Handel's *Messiah* can be heard everywhere.

Photo: The Weekly Packet

In many communities, groups go from house to house singing Christmas carols during the season. As Christmas falls in winter, they are warmly dressed.

Usually a big dinner makes its way to the family table sometime between 1 and 7 on Christmas Day. You, as a foreigner, for whom everyone will feel sorry if you are far from family, may well be invited to one of these. You may wish to bring a bottle of wine or champagne or flowers or a potted plant – the poinsettia is the Christmas flower.

NEW YEAR'S EVE Our calendar elects January 1 as the first day of the new year. The big celebrations are held the evening of December 31. Parties should be gala, and you are supposed to drink champagne and kiss everybody at midnight. Some of us prefer to go to bed at 11 p.m. and start the new year well rested, but the young and romantic feel that on this night of nights they must have a date and preferably be in love. New Year's Day, January 1, is subject to a round of Open Houses but can properly be celebrated very quietly – nursing a hangover or in making grandiose New Year resolutions (such as giving up smoking or losing weight).

The week before Christmas and New Year's Day is not a time anyone should seriously expect to get much business done. Those of your business partners who haven't flown to the homes of distant relatives may be in the mountains skiing or in the tropics swimming. Not everything grinds to a halt, but you are unlikely to find a full quorum of decision makers on the scene.

THANKSGIVING The fourth Thursday of November, Americans celebrate Thanksgiving and remember a supposed feast between the Indians and the Pilgrims in 1621. Had the Indians not befriended the Pilgrims during that winter, the Pilgrims would have starved. In recognition of this alliance (and ignoring all the bloodshed that followed) and of the success of the Mayflower settlement, Americans have a harvest feast.

Photo: Esther Wanning

The members of this family have flown in from all parts of the country to be together for Thanksgiving.

A big turkey (wild turkey was an Indian delicacy) is essential to Thanksgiving. Surrounding the turkey, you should see stuffing, cranberry sauce, potatoes, squash, and pumpkin and mincemeat pies. Whether or not the Pilgrims enjoyed the same foods, these dishes are all New England specialties that grace nearly every table at Thanksgiving.

It is as important to have somewhere to go on Thanksgiving as it is on Christmas. Some businesses are closed both on Thanksgiving, a Thursday, and the next day, a Friday, enabling people to travel great distances to join their families. However, other than wishing others a Happy Thanksgiving, Thanksgiving is not nearly as demanding as Christmas. No gifts or celebrating other than the dinner itself are required. It is a generous holiday, and many families welcome those who haven't a family of their own nearby.

The Minor Holidays

The significance of the minor holidays is mainly the long weekend they provide – many are observed not on their actual date but on a handy federally mandated Monday. A few of them are marked with parades, but the only celebration for most people is in sleeping late. Not all of them provide even that. On many of these holidays the ordinary worker works, but banks, schools, and government offices are closed. Stores are usually open and often have big holiday sales.

New Year's Day: January 1.

Martin Luther King Day: January 16, the birthday of the great civil rights' leader. The degree of observance varies from one city and state to the next. Often a school and government holiday, but most businesses are open.

Presidents' Day: The birthdays of Abraham Lincoln (February 12) and George Washington (February 20) are combined in one convenient mid-February Monday, awarding a welcome long weekend in the middle of winter. Theoretically, Franklin Roosevelt is included in the celebration, but few people realize it.

Valentine's Day: St. Valentine was the patron saint of lovers, and on February 14, people give cards, candy, and flowers to loved ones. Children often give cards to everyone they know. Not an official holiday.

Easter: A Christian holiday celebrating the day that Jesus rose from the dead. Children color Easter eggs and have Easter egg hunts and often receive chocolate bunny rabbits or baskets of candy and toys. The date falls on a Sunday anywhere between late March and late April. Easter heralds the beginning of spring.

Mother's Day: The second Sunday of May. A day to pay tribute to Mother, with cards, flowers, and restaurant dinners.

Memorial Day: On the last Monday of May; commemorates the Americans who have died in war and kicks off summer. A good day for a picnic.

Photo: The Weekly Packet

A Memorial Day parade in a small town brings out anyone who has served the country in the armed forces and still has a uniform to wear. Many flags are waved.

Father's Day: The third Sunday of June. Not as important as Mother's Day, but still the fifth largest card-sending occasion.

Fourth of July: On July 4, 1776, the Declaration of Independence was signed. Also called Independence Day, it's another good picnic day. Official celebrations consist of fireworks displays; most private fireworks are now illegal, but many people set them off anyhow.

Labor Day: The first Monday in September and the occasion for the last picnic of summer; a day of honor (and rest) for the worker. The school year traditionally starts a day or two after Labor Day.

Columbus Day: October 12, the day in 1492 when Columbus landed in the New World.

Halloween: October 31, the evening that children put on costumes and go out "Trick or Treating," which means that if you don't provide treats when they knock on your door, they will enact a dirty trick on you (such as writing on your windows with soap). It's a good idea to stock up on some Halloween candy (wrapped) to hand out, but you probably don't really need to worry about the tricks. It's the parents who do the worrying now – that some atrocious person will give their child poisoned food. For this reason, parents usually supervise their children's rounds very closely.

Veterans' Day: November 11. Honors those who have served their country in the armed services.

SPECIAL OCCASIONS

New Babies

It is customary for a friend to give a baby shower for an expectant mother. Traditionally, only other women are invited, and each arrives with a present for the baby, prettily wrapped. The usual routine is for the party to begin with refreshments and chat, followed by the opening of the presents. The women sit in a circle and the mother-to-be opens the presents one by one amidst oohs and aahs. Baby books, bonnets, little stretch suits, toys, blankets, and anything else a baby might want are all appropriate. A handmade item is especially appreciated.

There is no particular custom for visiting after the baby is born. Good friends might arrange to stop in a week or more after the birth, bearing a present if they haven't already contributed one at the shower. As new parents are harried and have little time to cook, they will be grateful if you bring them something for their dinner.

CHRISTENING A ceremony at which a baby is named and received into the church, usually as part of Sunday morning services. If you're invited to one of these, just do what everyone else does, and don't be insulted if you're not invited – usually only relatives are.

Birthdays

Except for children's birthday parties (see page 174), most birthday celebrations are kept within the family. Usually each family member gives a present to the birthday person. Children count on birthdays and Christmas as the times to get the big things they really want, such as new bicycles.

A home celebration consists of a special dinner, ending with ice cream and cake. For children, each candle on the cake represents one year of life, and everyone sings, "Happy birthday to you," when the cake appears, candles lit. The honoree then makes a wish and tries to blow out all the candles at once.

Weddings

The traditional American wedding was rocked by the sixties and emerged in a variety of new forms. It became popular for couples to write their own vows and to add a variety of personal touches to the proceedings. Nonetheless, many of the old customs survive, even if in an updated form, and some couplings are more tradition-bound than ever before.

The most important thing to know about weddings is that you must arrive on time. This is an occasion when the guests should appear before the hosts; it is most embarrassing to arrive after the bride has already walked down the aisle. As wedding ceremonies start on time and are usually very short, you may miss the main event entirely by being late.

THE CLASSIC CHURCH WEDDING When the American girl dreams of her wedding, she probably sees herself wafting down a church aisle on her father's arm, radiant in a long white dress.

You as a guest are occupying a pew in the church. When the processional music begins and the first members of the wedding party are visible, the congregation rises to its feet. Ushers, bridesmaids, and flower girls lead the procession, and the bride and her father bring up the rear. The groom, best man, and minister slip in quietly to their positions in front.

The minister begins, "Dearly beloved, we are gathered here together to join this man and woman in matrimony …" After his opening, the groom steps in to the father's place. (Modern variations remove the implication that the bride is a piece of livestock being given from the father to the husband.) Rings are exchanged – to be worn on the fourth finger of the left hand – and the ritual questions asked, "Do you take this man to be your husband/wife, to have and to hold, to love and cherish, in sickness and in health, till death do you part?"

By this time many in the audience are becoming weepy and getting out their handkerchiefs. The minister concludes with, "I now pronounce you husband and wife," the organist breaks into Mendelssohn's *Wedding March* and the happy couple sweeps joyfully back down the aisle, with the wedding party trailing afterwards.

The congregation departs, falling into the arms of long-lost relatives on the way out, and all go off to the reception.

THE VARIATIONS The above describes the standard Protestant ceremony. A Jewish service is somewhat different, and a Catholic Mass a great deal longer. Similar proceedings can take place in

Photo: Bambi Smith for Don Gerhardt Photography

At a formal wedding such as this, the bride and groom are "attended" by bridesmaids and ushers. It is an honor to be chosen to take part, one extended to brothers, sisters, and close friends.

gardens, homes, and hotels. Often a justice of the peace presides, removing the religious factor.

The simplest wedding of all is the City Hall version: the couple and a few witnesses appear before a judge and are married.

THE RECEPTION Here's where the money goes. There are means of spending lavish sums on a wedding reception. The caterers get the largest share, followed by expenditures for reception rooms, champagne, flowers, photographers, orchestra, printed napkins, and countless other little touches. Some families go into debt for years to pay off their daughters' weddings. (Tradition has it that the bride's family pays for the wedding, although increasingly – now that people wait longer to get married – couples finance and arrange their own.)

189

There is no disgrace, however, in a party at home with food supplied by the relatives. There are those who consider the small home garden party more charming than the no-holds-barred hotel affairs usually directed by a bossy photographer.

If there is a receiving line, etiquette demands that you pass through it. You kiss the bride (if you know her) and tell her she looks beautiful, and you shake the groom's hand and tell him he's a lucky man. You tell the bride's mother how moved you were by the ceremony, and you make a little joke to the bride's father about not having to pay his daughter's bills any more.

You have now done your duty and may drink champagne and circulate and join in the festivities, which usually start with food and drink and move on to dancing. When the orchestra strikes up, protocol demands that the bride and groom dance the first dance alone and the second with their parents. After the parents have danced, the rest of the guests may join in. When the word goes around that the bride and groom are going to cut the cake, everyone pulls close for a look at their first cooperative married venture. You must eat at least a bit of the cake for good luck.

Properly speaking, you should not nip out before the bridal couple does – although if it looks as if they're not going anywhere you needn't wait forever. The old standard is for the bride to disappear somewhere, then to reappear in her traveling clothes. Preferably from some balcony or staircase she throws her bouquet to a young unmarried woman – who may expect to be the next to be wed – and departs on the arm of her groom, amid showers of rice (a fertility rite). Today, however, many couples prefer to enjoy their parties to the end.

PRESENTS An old-fashioned custom is to display wedding presents received before the wedding at the reception, but most people do not consider showing off "the loot" entirely tasteful. You may bring your present to the wedding (it won't be opened until later), but most couples would prefer you mailed it to their home address.

Theoretically, one is allotted a year after the wedding in which to send a present, although most people don't wait that long. Cash is not quite as frequently given here as in some countries, although it is often most welcome. If you are uncertain, you might inquire from relatives as to the couple's wishes. Should the couple already have a house groaning with toasters and china, it may be there is nothing they would like better than money.

But cash (make it a check) should not be your first thought. The traditional wedding present is a handsome household item – anything from a good frying pan to a candelabra. Some brides register their desires at a prominent local store. Having found out where the bride is registered, you then need only appear there and pick out whatever is in your price range. Shopping at prominent stores in general has the advantage that the couple may easily return your present if they don't like it or if it's a duplicate.

Price should not be affected by the lavishness of the wedding reception – but often one can't help but feel that one should at least cover the cost of one's dinner. The real determinants of price should be your fondness and goodwill towards the couple, their needs, and how much you have to spend. A well-chosen gift of low cost will arouse delight among decent people. And if your own resources are small, the couple would feel badly should you spend more than you can afford.

If you are invited to a wedding and cannot attend, you are not obligated to send a present – although you may wish to. (You must, however, mail your regrets as soon as possible.) Likewise, if you receive an announcement after the fact of the wedding, a gift is entirely optional.

Quite promptly after sending your present, you should receive a thank-you note, giving specific and personal reasons as to why the couple was so delighted with your present. To not acknowledge a wedding present is unforgivable.

Funerals

These too come in a variety of forms. Most frequently, they are held in churches or funeral homes. You should wear somber, proper clothes (such as a dark suit with a sober tie for men and a prim dress or suit for women) and arrive looking reasonably solemn.

An usher will guide you to a seat. The service will probably be between a half-hour and an hour long. Many funerals now include testimonials from friends, but unless you have been solicited beforehand, you will not be required to speak, although you may be given the opportunity.

American funerals sometimes display an open casket and provide an opportunity for the attendees to file by and pay their last respects to the departed. You may find your friend remarkably changed in death, probably due to the activity of the morticians, who go to such lengths to make the dead face look serene that he or she may be unrecognizable.

During the funeral, you may sob all you like but you should not lose control or cry out loud. Unless you are next of kin, you do not wish to draw attention to yourself and your grief.

You may have an opportunity to greet family members after the funeral, whereupon you convey how sorry you are and how greatly the deceased will be missed. Sometimes there has also been an opportunity to call in at the funeral home on preceding evenings to console the family. There may be a graveside ceremony after the church service, which usually includes only family and close friends. Unless you are specifically invited, you should go home.

There may instead be a reception or a wake, likewise by special invitation. This may turn into a very jolly party, but you should try to do your part in keeping the focus on the departed – with stories and reminiscences of his or her uniqueness. It is sometimes hard to remember the sadness of the occasion when a number of long-lost friends and relatives gather together, and a certain amount of mirth is excused.

Death is not an occasion for monetary contributions to the family. Close friends and relatives may send flowers and wreaths for display at the funeral; often the family requests contributions to a certain charity instead.

If someone you know dies and you do not have an opportunity to speak to the bereaved family, you should write a note or send a sympathy card. Even if you attend the funeral, a note to family members reiterating your sorrow is thoughtful.

Dying

If you should suffer a death in your own family while in this country, be very wary of funeral homes, which are famous for charging astronomically for unnecessary services. Although it is not a time when one cares to be thinking about finances, it is unlikely that your loved one would wish you to bankrupt yourself after it is too late for him or her to enjoy the fruits of your spending. So think twice about whether you really need a mahogany, velvet-lined coffin, etc.

BANQUETS

All kinds of clubs and civic organizations find excuses to have banquets so you may well find yourself at one sooner or later. A banquet is usually held in a restaurant, but there the resemblance to a restaurant dinner ends. At a banquet, you're in someone else's hands and do what you're told.

A cocktail hour nearly always precedes dinner, which gives everyone a chance to gather together. "No-Host Bar" means you pay for your own drinks. An "Open Bar" provides free drinks. If you don't attend the cocktail reception, you probably won't be missed, but you should be on time for the dinner. Restaurant management sees to it that banquets begin on time.

Numerous, large round tables fill most banquet halls. Your place at one may be designated by a place-card (which you will have to search for) or you may have to find a seat of your own. If you don't know anyone, you want to cast your eye quickly around for people who at least look compatible, and then present yourself at that table and inquire if there is an empty chair. You will be expected to converse with your tablemates.

Sometimes the tablemates join in ordering bottles of wine, each person paying for a share. You will not have a choice of foods and don't expect any personal service. The group rate the organization enjoyed for the dinner was based on efficiency. Servers are capable of sweeping the meal on and off very quickly and hope you will not linger too long over your plate. The speech-making usually begins as soon as the coffee has come around, and any further clanking of cups and spoons should be subdued. Banquet speakers are generally forced to contain their remarks within strict time guidelines, but the social hour may go on after the meeting has officially adjourned.

If you are the honored guest, you will probably sit at the head table and not have to pay for your drinks. If you make a speech and people applaud, don't applaud back. You would then appear to be clapping for yourself. Just look gracious, allow a small smile to upturn your lips, and nod your head in acknowledgement.

GIFTS

Giving
Except for a few special occasions, Americans are not big gift-givers. Although a salesman may pass out free samples, there is no ritual exchange of presents among executives. In fact, if one American businessman were to give another a nicely wrapped present that had no bearing on the company's business, the recipient would consider the gift quite inexplicable, unless the object were valuable. Then the move could look like an embarrassing attempt at bribery. Even an inexpensive present could be taken as a slightly crass attempt to win somebody's consideration.

Americans have learned something of the role that gift-giving plays in certain other cultures, and when an American businessman goes to Tokyo, he goes equipped. But among ourselves, we don't see that we need presents. Presents cement the blossoming friendship among business partners, but as we don't need friendship to do business, we don't need presents either. We have contracts instead.

Even friends may never exchange presents. When I go abroad, I try to bring back little mementoes for close friends, but nobody would feel slighted if I didn't. I may occasionally buy a copy of a book for a friend, but I rarely remember a friend's birthday, and few people outside of family remember mine. If someone gave me presents too often I would think it tiresome, and I would feel the burden of having to reciprocate. Besides, like most Americans, I have plenty of stuff already.

However, a gift from a foreigner – suitably typical of his or her homeland – has greater dimensions than anything my fellow American could give me and won't go wrong, except to government employees who are prohibited from accepting gifts. Otherwise, don't hesitate to give small tokens to personal or business friends if you want to. But don't be insulted if you get nothing in exchange.

Receiving

One usually opens a present immediately and in front of the donor. (*Exceptions:* Christmas and birthday presents may be saved for the day, and wedding presents, as mentioned, are not opened at the wedding.) The best reaction is outright pleasure and delight at receiving something so lovely/indispensable/thoughtful. Show as much enthusiasm as possible and return to the subject periodically thereafter.

The donor will be particularly pleased if you emphasize that the gift shows his or her uncanny sensitivity to you and your tastes. ("How did you know that my old sugar bowl broke and that I collect Scottish china?" "Peonies are my favorite flowers!") It is not necessary to go on much about how the donor shouldn't have gone to all the trouble, etc. Too much of that and we begin to think maybe indeed we shouldn't have and become embarrassed that we did.

The Guest

You may want to bring a bottle of wine or flowers to a dinner party, but the practice varies in different social sets and you are never expected to. In more formal houses, the flowers may already be magnificently arranged, and your hosts do not at the moment of your arrival wish to go poking around the pantry looking for the right vase. Nobody will mind if you bring a nice wine, but your host is not obliged to serve it that evening. The grander the house, the less opportune a present is. After all, you wouldn't show up at the White House with a bottle of wine under your arm.

It is customary (although not obligatory) to bring something if you are going to be an overnight guest in someone's house. Some gourmet item, a good cheese, a present for the children – any little thing that shows your appreciation. It needn't be wrapped. You might also send a gift afterwards.

Christmas

Christmas accounts for most of the necessary gift-giving in this country. Children in many families receive presents only at Christmas and on their birthdays – but then frequently in great quantity. Some people give all their relatives presents; others only give to their immediate family. Children are expected to give as well as to get presents.

Some friends exchange presents at Christmas and some don't. Some instead give presents to the small children of friends. I usually keep a few spare presents on hand around Christmas of the generic type – candles, fruitcake – wrapped under the Christmas tree so that if people unexpectedly produce presents for me, I have something for them.

Christmas is the time to settle the score with anyone who has been helpful throughout the year. There are certain required cash outlays – to doormen, babysitters, house cleaners, newspaper deliverers – for anyone who has served you regularly (see "Tipping" in the Appendix for details). You might want to give a little something (not money!) to your children's teachers or to those among them who have especially extended themselves.

There is a considerable flow of liquor bottles during the holiday season. In business, Christmas presents are often a one-way street – the buyer gets the present. If a company has been favoring you with their business, you give. They don't need to give you anything; it's enough that they pay their bills.

Within the company, bosses may hand around gifts to their subordinates – or they may not. Many companies give a small Christmas bonus to all personnel. A hardworking secretary is often rewarded with something rather nice, and if the secretary is particularly fond of his or her boss, the boss may get a present too. It is unlikely that you need to provide presents for all your co-workers. Some departments have lotteries; a hat goes around with everyone's name in it, and you bring a small present to the Christmas party for the person whose name you drew.

Chapter Eleven

THE AMERICAN WOMAN

Just how liberated are American women? In theory, we are the equals of men in every way. Many foreigners think that American women are on top of the world. But in fact, any number of studies show that women, no matter how brilliant, are not taken as seriously as men. Furthermore, the average woman earns 70 cents for every dollar a man makes and does most of the housework too.

As a nation, however, we are committed to the equal rights of women. Jokes about women – as weak, flighty, bad drivers, extravagant, etc. – are considered tasteless. In the legal realm, there has been an enormous surge towards equality in the last twenty years. Employers who do not promote women now may get sued. The "Help Wanted" ads in newspapers used to be divided into columns for men and women, with clerical jobs for the women and managerial ones for the men. Now, a woman can aspire to nearly any job or training program. Women doctors, lawyers, and engineers are far more common than they were a few decades ago.

There are still not nearly as many women as men in the top ranks. A woman is a rare bird in the executive room of a corporation. A woman president of the USA is currently most unlikely, although a major party – the Democrats – ran a woman for vice president in 1988.

It is not solely discrimination that holds women back. Women remain accountable for the children, and the total commitment required for a high-powered career makes it very difficult to be a satisfactory mother too. Among executive women, 52% are unmarried.

Superwomen

The Superwoman Syndrome refers to the efforts of women to excel as worker, wife, and mother. The well-paid working mother can provide nannies as substitutes for herself, but she may not escape the guilt that comes from not spending more time with her children. The conclusion is always that no one can be Superwoman, although some women give it a jolly good try.

Even the ordinary working woman leads a life of ceaseless motion. She rises early, sees children off to school, and races out of the house to her job. She may commute a long way to work, perhaps dropping off a child on the way. Coming home, she picks up children, then does errands, cooks dinner, supervises play and homework, puts children to bed, and prepares herself for another day's work.

The average woman also feels the obligation to remain attractive and youthful, which requires hours devoted to exercise, beauticians, make-up, and shopping. The American woman often seems (or at least feels) less self-confident than her counterparts from other lands. She has spent an inordinate amount of her girlhood and her youth worrying about how to attract men, and her efforts have left her less natural than she might be otherwise. Eva Hoffman writes of the time and effort American girls expend on femininity. She herself, a Pole, "never thought you had to do anything special to be feminine – surely, it's enough to be a woman, isn't it?" Not in the American woman's mind, which is much affected by advertising.

When the women's liberation movement accelerated in the seventies, feminists hoped that the good female values would change the world for the better – businesses would become less competitive and more concerned with humane values, men would joyfully take on their share of childrearing, and women would no longer need to struggle to look like Marilyn Monroe. But on the contrary, women have instead molded themselves to fit into what is still regarded as "a man's world." You need only see the troops of women going off to work in their dark blue suits (indeed, with skirts, but with white shirts and neck scarves) to see that it's women who have done the adjusting.

The Foreign Man/The American Woman

To foreigners, American women may appear extremely free. The fact that American men help at all with housework shocks some. But the man who folds laundry and makes beds is not losing his manhood. When an American man goes out to find a wife, he is looking for a partner – someone with mutual interests, interesting conversation, an earning capacity, and a sense of humor. He can hardly expect his wife to be equal on most scores and inferior when it comes to washing the kitchen floor.

If you are a man from a country where women don't enter into men's territory, you may need to make an effort to treat women as equals. This means not asking the woman of the house about the children and then turning to the husband and saying, "And what do you think of the Russian peace initiatives?" Women think about these things too. You could find rewarding new realms of conversation opening to you.

Certainly you would not whistle at a woman, make lewd remarks, or try to hustle any stray woman off to bed.

A woman traveling alone, eating in a restaurant alone, or doing anything else alone may be very satisfied with her own company and not welcome intrusion (although she may be open to a tactful approach). She will certainly find very annoying any assumption that she is pining for a man.

There are now an abundance of women who have discovered that they prefer to be single. A single American woman has no obligation to stay home and look after aging parents and other people's children. Instead, she may have a wonderful career and an interesting life and count herself luckier than her married friends. One of the main disadvantages of being single is the attitude that such a woman must be a loser. She isn't.

— Chapter Twelve —

THE AMERICAN HOME

Let us take a little tour of a typical American home, a middle-class, middle-priced one in an average suburb. For all the differences among Americans, many of such houses across the country are remarkably alike.

We will arrive by car because there is no other way. As there is so little demand for one, no public bus comes down this street. Most of the families in this neighborhood have two cars, and a school bus may pick up the children.

The house we will visit is a one-story "ranch" house built in the sixties. We park directly in front, step out onto the sidewalk, and lock our car. It is midday, and there are no signs of people anywhere. Few people ever walk around here; there are no stores, restaurants, or bars within walking distance. If any of the neighbors were in their front yards, we would see them because there are few fences around the yards. A few shrubs separate one piece of property from another.

We walk up the front path. On either side of us is an expanse of green lawn, the weekend labor of the man of the house. Their lawn is part of the great lawn that spreads across America, cultivated on deserts, mountains, and seashores – a triumph over the wilderness. Few crops are more unnatural or more difficult to grow than a velvety green lawn, which must be planted, weeded, fertilized, watered, and cut regularly. By our lawns are we judged. Your neighbor may know nothing about you, but he will note the condition of your lawn.

Photo: Esther Wanning

This typical American ranch home could be found anywhere in the USA.

203

We push a button by the door and hear a ding-dong chiming inside. Very quickly someone answers. It is our host. Normally he and his wife would both be at work. Today is unusual. On a usual day he spends an hour getting to the city, traveling by car and train. His wife works in a nearby suburb, to which she drives.

The wife comes to greet us at the door. "Let's not stand around in the hall," she says. "Do come in." We follow the beige wall-to-wall carpeting into the living room, which is sparsely decorated with two white couches and several white easy chairs.

"Sit down and make yourselves comfortable," says our host. There are large color photographs of the children, framed in silver, on the walls, along with some framed museum posters. A glass coffee table has a copy of an immense book on it, *The Art of the Vatican*. There are no other books in this room. There are copies of *Time Magazine*, *National Geographic*, and *TV Guide* on the coffee table. A large unit on one wall encases a color television, a video cassette recorder, and a stereo.

The front curtains are always drawn because our hosts do not like the idea that someone walking by their house could see into their living room. However, the large side windows of the room let light stream in.

Electricity

We are served coffee, made in an electric coffeepot. Our hostess takes some chocolate chip cookies from the freezer and thaws them by putting them in the microwave oven for a minute. The electricity supply is very good and steady; there is rarely a power outage. You don't see any power poles outside because the power lines are buried underground.

If there were a power outage, this is what would stop working: the refrigerator, the freezer, the microwave oven, the clock radio, the televisions and stereo, the computer, the telephone answering machine, the doorbell, the garage door opener, the dishwasher, the clothes washer, the lights, the food processor, the electric blender, the electric toothbrush, and the air-conditioner. The burglar alarm has a battery backup so a thief cannot disconnect it by cutting the electrical wires to the house.

Climate Control

On hot days, the family closes the windows and doors and turns on the central air-conditioner. Cold air circulates throughout the house. Less modern houses have window air-conditioners, which only cool one room apiece. Some old houses and apartment buildings do not have adequate wiring to run air-conditioners, and a few people don't like them anyhow because of their noise and the artificial chill they produce. In the summer, open windows have screens in them, which keep flies and mosquitoes out.

In the winter, the central heating in this house can be counted on to heat all the rooms equally. In cold areas, storm windows are put up in the fall for insulation. The furnace is in the basement and vents in each room distribute the heat. Not driven together to heat themselves by a stove, family members may spend much of their time in the privacy of their own rooms.

House Tour

Foreigners often think it strange that Americans will show them every room of the house. "No wonder they don't want people dropping in," says an Irish woman, "when it means cleaning the entire house." But our hosts expect that we are curious to see everything, and they are rather proud of the size and decor of the bedrooms and of the pretty wallpaper in the bathrooms.

The dining room is an extension of the living room. We walk through it to see the kitchen, which is big and airy and sparkling clean. The appliances are all a matching cream color and look new. The refrigerator is six feet tall, defrosts itself, and produces ice cubes and ice water automatically. The kitchen has a glass door to the large backyard, which has a jungle gym in it that the children used when they were small. There is no swimming pool. This isn't Hollywood.

The other wing of the house has three bedrooms. As each of the two children has a room, and the parents the third, there is no guest room or study. But guests can sleep on one of the living room couches, which opens into a bed.

Each of the children's rooms is crammed with things: toys, games, a desk, a computer in one and a stereo in the other, stuffed animals, an encyclopedia, big posters of rock stars on the walls, a bookcase full of books. The older child has a telephone extension. There are in all four telephones in this house – two in bedrooms, one in the kitchen, and one in the hallway.

The parents' room is large, with a king-size bed and its own bathroom. There is another bathroom off the hallway, and each bathroom has a sink, toilet, and bathtub with shower. There are no bidets. The bathrooms are tiled and have pretty matching towels on the racks. If this were a newer, more luxurious house there would be even more bathrooms and perhaps a hot tub and jacuzzi (a large tub with swirling water) in the backyard.

There is no drain on the bathroom floor, and people who are bathing try not to splash. There's a bathmat folded on the side of a tub, which you put on the floor when you're taking a bath. You fill the tub, get in, wash and relax, then get out carefully and stand drying yourself on the bathmat. When you take a shower, you close the shower curtain, keeping its bottom side inside the tub to keep the water in. When you're finished, you turn the water off.

Americans would not think of instructing anyone in the use of the American toilet because we don't imagine that there is any other kind. Consequently, some foreigners have had interesting adventures with American toilets. To use, one pulls down one's pants and underpants (ladies pull up skirts) and sits down on the toilet, feet on the floor, facing the opposite wall. The toilet has a lid and a seat with a hole in it, and one sits on the seat rather than on the porcelain underneath. Toilet paper will be hanging within easy reach (one never needs to travel with toilet paper in America). When finished, one pushes a lever firmly in order to flush. Gentlemen urinate standing up and facing the toilet, having lifted both lid and seat. They should then return the seat to the lowered position before leaving the bathroom.

We leave the bathroom door slightly ajar and go next into the garage, where the family has fixed up a workshop. Far from being ashamed of manual labor, Americans take pride in being able to fix and make things. A man in particular likes to be "handy," and our host fixes broken chairs, changes electrical cords, and refinishes worn furniture at his workbench. Along the wall, there are shelves of leftover paint. The lady of the house has painted all the walls herself.

Not for the Ages

We think we could be comfortable here in this spacious, quiet house – at least for a while. It seems very anonymous, having been built from the same plans from which thousands of other houses across America were built. There was no attempt to make the house suit the landscape or the climate. The walls are not thick and sturdy; the doors are hollow. There is no wood trim or extra decor, the closets are small, and the ceilings are low. There is no fireplace. To many Europeans, these suburban houses are not well-built. The people who occupy them do not think of living in one place all their lives. They certainly don't expect that their children will grow up and stay in the same place. When people plan improvements, they often think more about what will increase the resale value than of what they themselves would most like.

Inside, there are no hidden nooks and crannies, no secret places, no signs of wear. The furniture is new; there are no family heirlooms and little that indicates the personalities of the occupants, despite their many interests. The house is so tidy that evidence of their hobbies is all hidden away.

Americans are consumers, not collectors. What happens to all the stuff they buy? Drive around on a Saturday or a Sunday and you will find garage sales. The family puts prices on their excess goods and sets them out in front of the garage. Everything from shoes that pinched to the old couch can be found for sale in a festive atmosphere, and if you like to bargain, this is your chance. Garage sales are a reasonable way for newcomers to furnish their houses. (You might also want to investigate resale shops, to which some people donate their used goods, if you're trying to set up housekeeping cheaply.) If you were to move here, you might have to get used to driving to the store every time you wanted a bottle of milk and to rarely hearing voices pass by and to having nobody ever drop in. But in time, you might find that you grew to like your privacy just as much as the people who live here now do.

Household Helpers

We rarely use the term "servants," a word that offends our ideas of democracy. They are house cleaners or housekeepers or babysitters or cooks – terms that imply some specialty other than being subservient.

American women have been lamenting the household help problem for generations, although there used to be a supply of immigrants or black women to do other people's housework. Then in World War II, the household helpers went off to work in the factories and afterwards never wanted to work in other ladies' houses again. And no wonder – the pay is bad, the employer can be difficult, and there are few benefits.

Most families are now accustomed to doing most of the household work themselves. Because so often both adults have jobs outside the home, professional families often have house cleaners who come in one or more times a week to do the general cleaning. But only very wealthy people still have cooks, gardeners, and daily housekeepers.

Consequently, families have found many shortcuts to make up for the fact that there is so often no mother who spends her day looking after the household. Breakfast may be a bowl of cereal, no one comes home for lunch, and dinner is often pizza or Chinese take-out food. There are numerous time-saving services, from plumbers who come in the evening to mail-order catalogs. Clothes are made of drip-dry fabrics or are sent to the dry-cleaners.

Americans are mad for time-saving devices, no matter how minuscule the time saved. Telephones with automatic dialing, microwave-ready meals, automatic watering systems, car telephones, central vacuuming systems, and electric garden clippers all give Americans the illusion that they may someday get time under control.

Nonetheless, the real work remains. The weekend for the typical hardworking family consists of shopping, cleaning, fixing things around the house, gardening, and an overall attempt to get ready for the next frantic week. Few people socialize much. Besides the various reasons taken up in chapters 9 and 10, there just isn't time.

Chapter Thirteen

DOING BUSINESS IN AMERICA

"The business of America is business," said President Calvin Coolidge in 1927. That statement is even more true today. Of all the ways to occupy one's time, work is the most important. Elsewhere, the sickness of a grandmother or the problems of a cousin would be reasonable excuses for taking a day off. Not so here. Nearly every other element of life is sacrificed before the work part.

Foreigners generally surmise that it's because "the dollar is king" that Americans are so work-crazy and that the unabashed fever for moneymaking overrides the finer feelings. There's some truth to this, but there's more than money driving the worker.

The Value of Work

A belief in progress, a sense of infinite resources, and an emphasis on tangible results contribute to unbounded enthusiasm for undertaking new projects. As an American's self-image is dependent on action, even wealth does not inhibit the work ethic.

To work well and hard is a high value. Although there are many who do neither, they are not the people who win the admiration of their peers, nor the ones who rise to the top. Those who want to command respect apply themselves diligently. No matter how splendid someone might be on other fronts, she does not wish to be thought remiss as a worker. Better to be labeled a bad daughter or thoughtless friend. Self-esteem is bound up in achievement, and when people lose their jobs or retire they often become depressed, even when money is not a problem. The more successful the person, the more likely it is that his life revolves around his or her career rather than around home and family.

A degree of unfettered ambition, one that might even be found gauche in other countries, is admired here. An Englishman would not care to be known as "all business." An American would. At the bottom of the career ladder, where people serve fast food for minimum wage, people work hard, but the job does not overlap into leisure hours. The higher one rises, the more all-consuming the job becomes.

Company Operations: The Bottom Line

The company is in business for one reason: to make a profit for the owners – individuals or stockholders – and to make more profit than could be made if the capital were invested otherwise. This is not so simple as many businesses are up against cutthroat competition and must keep prices low or lose market share.

This single-minded dedication to profits leads to ruthless operations. American companies are quick to throw out the old and bring in the new. Typically, they make only short-range plans and

211

want fast profits. Since the eighties, when the USA became the world's biggest debtor nation, more and more companies have felt under siege. Publicly held companies are subject to unfriendly takeovers. Most companies do not feel stable enough to make their workers too comfortable, and job security is not a feature of American worklife.

In countries such as Japan, social benefits are part of corporate philosophy; companies factor in the higher costs of keeping everyone employed and using goods made at home, etc. The extra costs are paid for through higher consumer prices. The American viewpoint is that the citizen/consumer, who is also the worker, is best served by the lowest prices. In the process workers may lose their jobs, but the deserving will find other ones. Thus by an "invisible hand," the economy is directed to function in the most efficient manner – at a cost of much upheaval and dislocation.

The Job Hop

As companies are constantly reorganizing, retrenching, and being bought and sold, they have many occasions to lay off workers. They may do so regretfully, but they feel no compulsion to go on supporting the unprofitable employee.

The workers on their side are always free to improve their situation by looking out for new jobs and are quick to move if a better opportunity presents itself. Were company fidelity alone to cause someone to reject brighter prospects, her colleagues would probably think her stupid. After all, someone who doesn't move voluntarily may end up moving involuntarily.

Manual workers, however, currently have limited options because so many manufacturing jobs have been lost in the past decade, and the new service jobs are badly paid. The federally mandated minimum wage rises to $4.35 on April 1, 1991, a figure that leaves the worker worse off than she was twenty years ago.

Executives

Life at the top is very different from life at the bottom, except in one regard – it can be just as insecure. Mistakes are not easily forgiven, and even a long-time employee in the highest ranks can be summarily dismissed. (Those at the top, however, will probably leave with a very handsome severance package, whereas lower down, a few weeks' pay may be the most the worker can hope for.) Those closely associated with the ousted executive may be out the door as well, leading to Byzantine politics in which underlings try to keep lines of communication open to several factions within the company.

Democracy does not figure largely in the American corporation. Important decisions are made at the top, usually in secrecy, and based on a heavy weight of facts and figures. The chief executive officer may take complete responsibility for a key decision after thrashing it out in executive meetings.

As few people are involved, a decision in the USA can be made quickly. However, it may take longer to implement than in a system in which everyone was involved beforehand in making the decision. If a venture goes bad, the person who championed it can be fired, which would not occur where there is consensus management. The person fired could be the chief executive officer.

Business life is tense. Few American companies can stand still and reap the rewards of past success. The tempo of change is too fast, products become obsolete overnight, and the time between the introduction of a new product and acceptance by the public is astonishingly short. In 1981, few Americans knew what a VCR was. By 1989, 66% of American homes owned one. The executive who is trying to keep his company prosperous in such fast-moving times is not in a position to relax.

Executive Life

For his trouble, the fellow (it almost certainly is a man) at the top is extremely well compensated. The differential between top and bottom salaries in the USA is far greater than in most developed nations. It is not unusual for top executives to collect millions of dollars a year in pay, stock options, and bonuses. In the last decade, while executive remuneration rose, taxes in the highest income bracket went down. Millionaires are now commonplace.

Amiability is not a prerequisite for rising to the top, and there are a number of chief executive officers with legendary bad tempers. It is not the boss's job to worry about the wellbeing of his subordinates (although the man with many enemies will be swept out more quickly in hard times); it's the company he worries about. His business savvy is supposed to be based on intimate knowledge of his company and the industry so he goes home nightly with a full briefcase. At the very top – and on the way up – executives are exceedingly dedicated.

The American executive must be capable of enough small talk to get him through the social part of his schedule, but he may not be a highly cultured individual. Although his wife may be on the board of the symphony or opera, he himself has little time for such pursuits. His reading may largely concern business and management (American companies are often trendy in their attempts to keep up with the latest innovations in business methods), despite interests in other fields. Golf provides him with a sportive outlet that combines with some useful socializing.

These days, he probably attempts some form of aerobic exercise to "keep the old heart in shape" and for the same reason goes easy on butter and alcohol, substances thought to contribute to making highly stressed executives suddenly drop dead. (These health endeavors may be favorite conversational subjects.) But his doctor's admonition to "take it easy" falls on deaf ears. He likes to work. He knows there are younger men nipping at his heels. Despite the occasional newspaper article about the executive who gives up the rat race, few actually are eager to be put out to pasture.

They may, however, be quite willing to move on to greener

pastures. Corporate headhunting, carried on by "executive search firms," is a growth industry. America has great faith in individual talent, and dynamic, aggressive executives are so in demand that companies regularly raid each other's managerial ranks.

Employee Life

"In Argentina I worked just as hard," an Argentinian architect complained, "but work wasn't as stressful or competitive as it is in the USA. There you feel part of a group that helps each other, but here you feel disposable."

Foreign employees of American companies sometimes feel the lack of spoken praise, which is often felt to be superfluous here. Good work is noted and rewarded with salary increases and promotions. Bad work is usually quickly brought to the employee's attention.

Competitive tension here goads the workers on, but it also causes a high level of anxiety. When results are quantifiable, many companies give awards to the most productive workers, thus pitting one worker against another. While there's always some give and take among people who work together, individual effort prevails over teamwork, and the level of trust in an office may be low.

Company loyalty is also rather slight, and people identify themselves by kind of job ("I am a bank manager") rather than by company name. Co-workers may speak very derisively of the company among themselves ("Thank God it's Friday and I'm outa here"), although it's understood that this doesn't affect the quality of their efforts. Within the company, while one might have some loyalty to one's manager, one would not be expected to put one's own job on the line for him or her. It is to yourself that you are expected to be true.

Despite the stress level, many foreigners find the American work climate very satisfying, particularly ambitious people who felt stymied in their own cultures. "America is the best place for work," says an English woman, now staying home with her baby. "Working so hard was very stimulating, and I found my job exciting and rewarding." Even many of those who complain about the relentlessness of the pace admit they would be bored in a more restful atmosphere.

Hiring

The process of interviewing and hiring for job vacancies usually is an even-handed one. If no one is on the spot for an opening, the company lists it in the newspaper, or with an employment agency, and waits for resumés to roll in.

Candidates with the most promising records are invited in for interviews and get a chance to demonstrate ease of manner, enthusiasm, and ideas. This is not the moment for undue modesty (although one should not sound like an unbearable braggart). There are many books of advice for the job seeker, and the newcomer to America would be wise to consult the literature. By law, women and minority applicants must be given equal consideration.

Although connections are not necessary even for the best jobs, the person who comes recommended has an edge. However, in the end, nobody will hire you just because you are so-and-so's niece or nephew. Even if you are, your qualifications will have to be at least as good as the competition's. In some cases, a relationship could be a drawback as nepotism is looked on unfavorably.

Despite the opinion of many business journalists that the MBA's (persons holding degrees in business administration) are wrecking American business with their narrow, methodical, cold-blooded methods, and although they are disdained by many old-line entrepreneurs, these MBA's are much in demand and those from the elite schools start with very high salaries.

Personnel Policies

Company employment policies are nearly all neatly codified and presented to the new employee at the time of hiring. Although a company has the fundamental right to dismiss an employee at any time, recent lawsuits have caused most companies to carefully document the procedure leading to firings.

Work hours, vacation time, coffee breaks, pension plans, sick leave, and rights are itemized and administered with impartiality. No matter if one person has a dying mother, and another develops disabilities. Mitigating factors may be tolerated for a time, but the employee who can't meet the standards can expect eventually to be dismissed.

There are, of course, plenty of exceptions to the impersonal approach and many cases of companies that have stuck by their workers through thick and thin. But even then, the bosses will probably excuse themselves by saying, "She was too good a worker to lose. We knew she'd be back some day." Whether true or not, nobody would want to admit that a business decision had been tilted by purely human considerations.

Office Relationships

Most offices are informal, with lots of joking around, back-slapping, and breeziness. Office doors are usually left open, unless a meeting is in progress. Although everybody knows perfectly well who the boss is – and subtly jockey for attention – the deference paid is less obvious than in more hierarchical societies.

For many people, the workplace becomes a substitute for the community that is fast disappearing from urban life. It's in the office that gossip, recipes, and names of barbers are exchanged and where someone will listen to how your date went last night. The department will take you out to lunch on your birthday and send you flowers when you're bereaved. The young and single may drink together, rent ski cabins in the winter, and set up blind dates for each other.

Nonetheless, it's a transitory community. Few groups stay intact for long. The members bond together for a while, but the ties are

Department meetings can be very informal.

fragile and often don't outlast a regrouping. Americans are good at the quick relationship – thick today, gone tomorrow. After all, in the course of a career, a vast number of paths cross, and it would be impossible to keep up with all of them.

Managers do not routinely involve themselves in their subordinates' personal lives. They may indulge in some friendly chat on personal subjects, but they do not consider themselves responsible for anyone's emotional wellbeing. This is not pure hardboiled indifference but reflects also the respect for privacy which so often in American life takes primacy over other needs. The American viewpoint is that the worker has a right to conduct his personal life however he sees fit as long as it does not affect his job performance. Despite the separation of job and life, many workers keep pictures of wives, husbands, and children on their desks, a practice some foreigners find very odd.

Initiative Before Deference

The hierarchy is not rigid in most offices. Managers encourage ideas from subordinates, and subordinates feel free to contradict their superiors. Promotion is by no means orderly, and tomorrow you may be reporting to someone who reported to you yesterday.

It doesn't hurt to be pushy and aggressive (within reason). The theory is that if you're aggressive in your own cause, you'll exert yourself for the company too. You can also get away with stepping on a few toes on the way up, although it's well to cultivate supporters as well.

One large California computer company runs a special course for its Asian-born employees, a course popularly known as "rudeness training." The intent is to teach those from non-confrontational cultures how to be direct and assertive – to clients, co-workers, and to their own bosses.

Corporate Cultures

According to the *Economist Business Traveller's Guide* to the United States (an invaluable book in supplying both insight and specific city information), office atmospheres vary from coast to coast. New York is frenetic, pressured, and more formal than elsewhere; the Midwest is conventional and methodical; the West Coast allows a degree of nonconformity. But you can also expect to find laid back offices in New York and formal ones in Los Angeles. Even in Midwestern Chicago, you'll come across eccentricity.

Beyond locale, particular companies are known for distinctive "corporate cultures." There are those that pride themselves on creating a family atmosphere and provide employees with unusual security. IBM, long a subject of mirth because of the regimentation of its employees, recently offered irresistible retirement packages rather than lay off any employees. Many companies run bowling leagues and baseball teams, and on weekends the employees' children paddle in the company pool.

Some companies make a point of giving employees an enormous amount of autonomy ("We don't care what you do or how you do it – just get results"). There are companies that emphasize creativity, and others that are very disciplined; some have rigid chains of command and others almost imperceptible chains. Many, goaded on by those books and courses on management, are constantly dreaming up new ways of organizing and issuing new work flow charts.

The human factor may anywhere override a particular company's stance. The manager of one department in a company may develop strong team spirit, whereas another whips up a deadly competition. In the end, however, both managers must produce results.

DOING BUSINESS WITH AMERICANS

Get to the Point

By all reports, the single greatest difference between business dealings in the USA and the rest of the world is the American eagerness to get to the point. Most peoples of the world don't negotiate with strangers. Therefore the first order of business is to get to know their callers, no matter how long it takes. Then they can decide if these are people they want to work with.

All this is a mystery to an American. Why sit around jawing and drinking cup after cup of coffee when you could be making deals? Certainly we want to know if you can deliver, the strength of your company, your resources. Why don't you tell us that instead of about the beauty of T'ang Dynasty vases? Then we can get down to how much, when, and who pays for what. At the end of several days when the American realizes that he and his new friends haven't yet lighted on one significant aspect of the business he came to talk about, he's ready to exit by the nearest window.

It's not that we're automatons. We're friendly, and we want to be liked. We're glad to have a little let's-all-relax chitchat at the beginning of a meeting. We'll even occasionally offer you coffee, if the company coffeepot isn't too far away. We'll take you out to lunch, but by the main course we expect to have the pleasantries out of the way and got down to brass tacks. We just don't think it's necessary to know someone very well to do business with them. After all, if we find we don't like you after we've done a little business, we can dump your company and try a different one.

Another reason that we want to get on with the business at hand is that it's what interests us. Whereas business people from other countries may be frankly bored with business and prefer to talk about other things, Americans are not. It's abstract conversations that bore us; the pragmatic American likes a conversation that is going somewhere. Stuck making small talk for hours, we're like racehorses shut up in the paddock. We long for a chance to show our stuff.

Tick Tock

In the mind of the American business person the clock is always ticking, and there are further worlds to conquer. Why spend any more time than necessary on this deal? We feel no need to be soulmates. We are not going to base this relationship on trust anyhow. We are going to base it on an elaborate, detailed contract which our lawyers will draw up.

During the workday, Americans are very precise about time. If you're ten minutes late for an appointment, you should apologize. If you're half an hour late, you should have a good reason. When you see your American host drumming his fingers and looking at his watch, wrap up the meeting quickly. And don't be insulted if he announces he has another meeting and unceremoniously turns you out of his office. Very likely he does have another meeting, and he has to be there on time. It doesn't mean that he's any less interested in your business.

221

Making Contact

As anywhere, when you're trying to get in the door it helps to have mutual acquaintances. But if you don't, the formal approach is perfectly acceptable. Find out who is in charge of the area of your interest and write a letter, in English, typed, stating your credentials and intentions. You may want to open negotiations at the top, by having your president contact the American company's president.

If you don't get a reply, follow up with another letter or a phone call. It's helpful to have an exchange of correspondence before you arrive for a meeting so the Americans can consider your proposal and involve the right people.

If you're flying in for a meeting, be sure you have an appointment before you arrive. Americans keep tightly packed schedules, and should you arrive without appointments, you could discover that your important contacts have absolutely no time to see you.

Meetings

A lot of business decisions are made in meetings, which can be stormy. Those in attendance are expected to bring up objections, thrash out problems, and defend their positions. Those in a losing position are not supposed to brood about loss of face.

To many foreigners, the American approach is cold and rational; we like a proposal that is based on facts and figures. Our main interest is price, and we are incredulous to hear that in some cultures the business relationship is more important than the price.

Americans will appreciate it if you show up at a meeting armed with all the pertinent statistics and deliver a well-rounded pitch, including the data that proves what a great company you represent. It's a good idea to work in how great you are too, although you must be a little more offhand in forwarding yourself. Americans accept arrogance, but too much boasting can arouse doubts. "Doing business is completely different here," says a Japanese businessman. "I make my presentation, they ask questions and I'm done."

We favor fast-talking, smooth operators, which is why some of our most successful envoys fail in countries where fast talkers are distrusted. Humility goes a lot further outside the United States. The important thing here is to make it clear that you are a "can-do" kind of person and that you understand what the Americans want.

Straightforwardness

Americans do not appreciate being "strung along." If, as is done in some countries, you offer pleasant reassurances that turn out not to be true, American business people will be highly annoyed – "Why the devil didn't someone tell us?" We want the straight scoop, the real story. If you can't deliver when you said you would (and June 1 means June 1, not sometime in June) tell us now so we can plan for it. We'll still like you better than the bunch who couldn't deliver and didn't tell us.

Those from the Far East may be shocked by the bluntness with which an American reports negative news. "Sorry, but we got a better price from someone else," or "Those blouses were badly made." In another culture your feelings would be considered more important than the truth, whereas we consider that we're doing you a favor by our straightforwardness. Now you know why you're not getting our business and can do something about it. And we've saved you from wasting your time in anticipation. But this can seem very cold-hearted in some cultures.

Accountability

You may find the decision-making process fairly streamlined in an American company, compared to that in other countries. Certain key decisions will probably require an executive board's approval, but very often there are somebodies along the line with the authority to make lesser decisions. Who these people are is generally not a secret.

Business Entertaining

Americans can be lavish entertainers. We see the value in breaking bread with our counterparts from other countries and most executives have quite decent expense accounts, but few would care to be out every night. If you find yourself less royally entertained than in some other countries, it could be because most Americans prefer a steak and salad themselves to what they regard as the tedium of a five-course meal in a French restaurant.

As conversation isn't our favorite indulgence either, we assume that you too would be as glad to lie down and take off your shoes as to be dragged all over town. So a night out with American hosts will probably not be excessively long. Americans do not consider that their manhood requires them to sacrifice sleep.

If you are traveling with your spouse, be sure that your host knows it so that he or she won't be left out of evening plans. If the American wives (or husbands) don't appear, it is probably because they a) have business of their own; b) live in a distant suburb to which your host will be returning on the late train; c) can't find a babysitter; or d) are bored stiff by business dinners.

Breakfast and Lunch

You may find yourself facing the business breakfast, favored by Americans who don't want to break up the business day, or who don't have enough lunches on their calendars to go around. If the thought of bacon and eggs at eight in the morning makes you sick, just have a roll and coffee. The point of the business breakfast is not to eat breakfast.

Lunches don't often last for much over an hour. Americans have never had the tradition of the long midday repast, and the practice of having a few drinks with lunch is fast disappearing. At breakfast and lunch, the Americans will expect to talk business for at least part of the time; dinner can turn out to be purely social, particularly if couples are involved.

The person who did the inviting does the paying. If your hosts took you out the first time, you may wish to reciprocate and invite them the next. The *Economist Business Traveller's Guide* to the United States supplies excellent recommendations for restaurants in major US cities.

Names, Rank, and Titles

Nearly everybody these days is on a first-name basis. If you prefer some other form of address, say so. One Japanese man, who after twelve years here still can't get used to strangers calling him by his first name, gives out his last name by itself, which Americans think is his first name.

Titles don't matter much in the business world. It's important to know who the company president is, but you wouldn't call him "President Watson." If you're not using a first name, say Mr., Mrs., Miss, or Ms. (See "What Do I Call You?" on page 150.)

You do need to know who the important people are at the meeting or else you may find yourself addressing your remarks to the distinguished looking older man who turns out to be the company bookkeeper rather than to the awkward-looking kid who happens to be the chief executive officer. Try to listen carefully when the introductions go by. Of course, even in America, there's enough homage paid to the boss so that observers don't have to be too brilliant to figure out who counts.

Business Cards

Cards play a minor role in American business and may not come out until the end of a meeting. They are used mainly to pass on an address and phone number, not as credentials. Most people have them, however, and you should too, printed in English.

Dress

Unless very sure of themselves, gentlemen visitors will probably do best to wear the kind of conservative suits that Brooks Brothers and Paul Stuart are known for: grey or dark blue, understated and well-made. Nothing should be polyester or shiny, and the cut should be classic and conservative. Subtle tweeds are fine; pinstripes must be very narrow, barely perceptible as stripes. In the summer, a cotton khaki suit will do, although if you have a little panache you might get away with wearing seersucker.

You're safest in a white or light blue shirt. Drip-dry is acceptable as long as the naked eye can't tell the difference. Colored shirts with white collars are too trendy. A tie cannot be flamboyant, and any bright colors should be discreet. The pattern should be small, as in little dots or vague stripes. Never wear jewelry.

Black wing-tip shoes are favored among conservative dressers, although loafers will probably not shock anyone. Belts should be black.

These guidelines are merely starting points. California computer types and Texas oilmen allow themselves remarkable liberties, and when you know with whom you're dealing you can adapt. However, the above wardrobe will establish you as safe and trustworthy anywhere.

Women are allowed more color and variations. Some executive women disdain suits in favor of colorful skirts or dresses (often worn with a jacket), but if you want to be entirely safe, a suit, worn with a dressy blouse and a scarf around your neck, will take you anywhere. Pants will not do, even in a pantsuit, at least not until you've examined your American counterparts. In the winter, boots are ideal footwear, and in summer, shoes with thick heels – rather than spikes – are preferable for anyone with much walking to do.

Photo: Kristy MacDonald

The beard and the loafers distinguish this executive from the total corporation man, but his look is nonetheless respectable – white shirt and pinstriped suit.

Gifts

Forget about graft. No respectable business greases palms. (Yes, there are occasional scandals involving the government, but they're far outside the norm.) An American who found that someone had left him a briefcase full of money would be struck dumb. Even gifts are unusual, except at Christmas. (See "Gifts" on page 194.)

Business Hours

The standard working day is 9 to 5, although for executives those are minimal work hours. On the West Coast, working hours are often 8 to 5, and anyone in the West doing much business with the East has to get an early start. West Coast stockbrokers are at work by 6 a.m. (when it's 9 a.m. on the New York Stock Exchange). Some cities with major traffic problems encourage flexible work hours ("flex-time") so that within one company some people might work from 7 to 3 and others 10 to 6.

Americans do try to keep their weekends for home and family. You might, however, be invited to someone's home on the weekend for a dinner, barbecue, or brunch.

Some urban dwellers have weekend homes in the country and leave early on Fridays to get to them. It is a very favored guest who is invited to the country home. If you are so honored, write a thank-you note to your hostess afterwards.

Vacations

American vacation time is extremely short compared to European and even many Asian allotments. It increases with length of employment; most people qualify for only a couple of weeks a year. Eventually, some may receive a month's vacation, but usually take a week here and a week there, being loath to leave their offices for a month at a time. Because of the children's school holidays, summer is the commonest time for a break.

Frequently (life speeds up in more and more ways), people make the most of long weekends rather than take substantial vacations. Supposedly, fear of what will happen in their absences causes many people to settle for four-day holidays – just long enough for the New Yorker to fly down to the Caribbean.

Communicating

Americans are expected to answer their mail and they'll expect you to answer yours. If you don't, you'll be thought unreliable. So even if you don't have an immediate answer, it's best to write and say so. Letters can be very brief.

The telephone is heavily used. Many, many questions that would call for a personal meeting in another country are resolved over the phone here. We can happily do business with people we have never met at all.

Secretaries

Persons of importance have a personal secretary who take care of their appointments and correspondence and who is a buffer between the person and those demanding to see him or her. It's helpful if the secretary likes you, and you should learn his or her name. Although the secretary probably doesn't influence major decisions, he or she can forward your cause in various ways, not the least of which is in putting your phone calls through.

Women in Business

Although few women have arrived in executive boardrooms, they are fast on their way up the ladder. Among corporate managers, 36% are women, and chances are good that your visiting foreign team will be meeting women who are doing the same job they are.

Some foreigners are not used to negotiating with women, but they should try to acclimatize very quickly or risk badly antagonizing a prospective business partner. Be sure that you are not in the habit of assuming that all women are secretaries.

Photo: Kristy MacDonald

The well-dressed businesswoman – a woman's clothes need not be as subdued in design or color as a man's.

The correct procedure is simple: treat a woman as you would a man. This does not mean that you can't discreetly help her on with her coat after a business lunch, but you should ask her the same questions you would a man and give the same regard to the answers.

Allow a woman to pick up the check under any circumstances when a man in her position would pay. Don't take over in restaurants if she invited you; she understands a wine list. Do not be overly solicitous of her safety – she's used to going home alone in a cab. And do not, under any circumstances, make a pass at her unless you want to see your whole deal go up in a puff of smoke.

The truth is that it is tough for a woman in a man's world. One reason is that the one endeavor that society takes as seriously as "worker" is "mother," and the working mother constantly feels she is cheating either her job or her children. (The working father can be regretful he sees his children so little, but he isn't considered a bad father.) She will appreciate it if you don't make her job any harder for her. If working with women is a new experience for you, you may be pleased to discover what a pleasure it can be. Even in America, many women insist, to get ahead they must be twice as good as a man.

CULTURE SHOCK

My own experiment with culture shock came to an abortive end when I returned prematurely and gravely homesick from a year's study in Italy. I had never heard of culture shock. All I knew was that I was unhappy and wanted to go home.

That was twenty years ago, and since then culture shock has become a bona fide field of study. It is now understood that any normal person, finding him or herself for an extended time in a new culture, is in for trouble.

After all, our ideas on how to behave were formed in our early years. Nobody explained that we were learning standards applicable only in our own culture, that across the border things were done differently. We were taught that we were learning how to do things right. Consequently, when we turn up in a foreign land, the ways of others look simply wrong.

Even more difficult is that we frequently don't discriminate between cultural problems and personal ones. If an American sees you in the street and doesn't stop to talk, you may think he is rude. But he's not; he's just in a hurry, and he expects you to understand that being on time matters. But if you haven't learned about American values, you may find yourself feeling very disoriented. Left and right, people are behaving in ways you find unpredictable. Something seems terribly wrong, but you don't know what it is. Like me, you may just want to go home.

The Honeymoon
The process of "culture shock" is now recognized as so predictable that its four stages have been codified. The first is the "honeymoon" stage, familiar to those of us who love to travel but never stay in one

place long enough to find out what follows. In the honeymoon stage, the new country and its people seem delightful. Better than home. Everything is so different and charming, the people so nice, the customs so interesting. This stage lasts a month or two.

All At Sea

Then the bloom comes off the rose. Now the people start to look shallow, selfish, stupid. The different ways of doing things don't seem interesting any more – just wearing. You start to feel tired all the time. Culture shock has set in. You feel at sea. What are you doing in a place like this?

This response, stage two, could not be more natural. You are surrounded by people who grew up absorbing this culture, and you don't know how to do simple things. Even if you speak the language, you simply cannot understand the way the people behave. You don't feel you can be yourself around them. A sense of loss grips you. After all, you have lost a part of your identity, that self who back at home was confident and masterly.

The emotional response to culture shock can be extreme. Confusion, depression, anxiety, and resentment can all enter to varying degrees. You may become physically ill. Little things seem terribly annoying. A perceived insult reduces you to tears.

At this point, many foreigners are tempted to retreat to an enclave of foreigners. Because there are so many immigrants in the USA, it is usually not hard to find companions from your homeland. They can be a great comfort, but also a danger.

If your fellow emigres steadily reinforce your negative feelings about Americans, you are less likely to overcome your culture shock. Rather than adjusting, you may move into a sub-community of foreigners, and Americans will remain ever-strange to you. The shock may wear off, but you are still uncomfortable and homesick.

Adjusting

The happier resolution is to move on to stage three. The old hands among your countrymen reassure you that they once felt as you do now. Rather than itemizing what's "wrong" with Americans, you remind yourself that "right" and "wrong" are not meaningful terms in cultural matters.

Instead, you try to understand what motivates Americans, perhaps realizing that many of the things you don't like are related to the things you do like (such as weak family ties and freedom; the fast pace and opportunity). Seek out Americans and ask them questions about the things that confuse you. They will be flattered.

If you try to keep an open mind, take the time to learn about America, and mix with Americans, your prognosis is good. It's important in this stage not to stay at home and mope but to get out and find things you like to do – whether going to the park, exploring, taking classes, playing soccer, or visiting flea (second-hand) markets. And keep on studying the language.

Acceptance

Within six months or a year of arrival – longer for some people – you should be moving into stage four, which is acceptance. At this point, you simply don't think much any more about the peculiarities of Americans. You accept them as individuals.

You have started to feel at home; you know how to do things. You have discovered that it is possible to be a bicultural person. You have not rejected your old culture; but the American ways have settled upon you. You feel optimistic about your future here. You should. You have truly arrived.

CULTURAL QUIZ

Here follow a few situations over which some foreign visitors have been known to stumble. What would *you* do?

SITUATION 1

You are a man employed by a large company, and many of your co-workers are women. Where you come from, strong barriers separated men and women, and you find you really like the looseness between the sexes here. To show how much you like working with women, you:

A Touch them often, draping an arm around the ladies' shoulders or taking hold of a hand or arm.

B Compliment the women constantly on their hair, clothes, and pretty smiles.

C Compliment your female colleagues on their good work.

Comments

Although a lot of contact is permissible between men and women in this society, the office is not a dating situation, and women should be treated professionally. Too much of *A* could get you in hot water; you could even face charges of sexual harassment. *B* will simply be found annoying. *C* will be pleasing to one and all.

SITUATION 2

You want to have a telephone installed quickly at your new apartment. You should:

A Call the telephone company and accept the first appointment for installation that you're offered.

B Appear in person at the telephone company's offices and explain how important it is that you get a phone promptly.

C Find someone with connections to the phone company who can see that you go to the top of the list.

Comments

A is all you need to do. Most businesses serve their customers impartially on the basis of first-come, first-served. Your phone is likely to be installed within a week.

SITUATION 3

A friend has invited you to dinner at a nice restaurant. You dine well, and at the end the waiter brings the check and puts it in the middle of the table. You expect your friend to pick up the check, but he (or she) doesn't. You wait, and the conversation grows slow, and still he (she) doesn't. You are getting very tired and are beginning to think that he expects *you* to pick up the check. What do you do?

A Grit your teeth and wait some more.

B Pick up the check and pay it.

C Pick up the check and say, "Shall we split it?"

Comments

C is the most reasonable course of action. You could also just produce your share of the check, based on what you ate and drank.

You may have been justified in expecting him to pay, particularly if he selected the restaurant. But people often propose meals together without intending to pay for the other person. If your friend happens to be a client of yours, he might be hoping you'll pay, but if the dinner was his idea he should not expect you to. Unless you're very sure someone is paying for you, take enough money to cover dinner when you go out.

SITUATION 4

In the college cafeteria, you meet an American and fall into a long and revealing conversation. You are new in the USA and lonely. Here, you think, is a real friend. You exchange phone numbers, but your new friend doesn't call. The following week, you see her again in the cafeteria, but although she smiles and says "hi" in a friendly way, she passes by your table to sit with other people. You feel very hurt. What has happened?

A She found out more about you and decided not to pursue the friendship.

B Much as she enjoyed the conversation, it wasn't necessarily meaningful to her. The rapport the two of you quickly achieved does not make her think of you as a special friend, and having an intimate conversation does not commit her to future closeness.

C She has so many intimate conversations that she has forgotten all about this one.

Comments

B is the most probable answer. You'll have to build up more of a shared history before you become anybody special to her. Why don't you call her? This may prove to be a real friendship some day; it just isn't one yet. C is a possibility as well.

SITUATION 5

A friend is visiting your house when the phone rings. It is someone you don't hear from often and you are anxious to catch up on news. What should you do?

A Ignore the visiting friend in favor of the telephoning one and have a nice, long chat. Apologize when you hang up.

B Express your happiness at hearing from the caller, then explain that you have company and ask when you can return the call.

C You shouldn't have answered the phone at all.

Comments

Either *B* or *C*. Not answering the phone is easier if you have an answering machine. A live visitor should always take precedence over the one who dropped in by phone. As Americans allocate their time carefully, they will resent their visiting time with you being idled away while you talk to someone else. Even if there are other people around to entertain, guests will not like being treated as second fiddles.

SITUATION 6

While visiting the USA on business you would like to make contact with Company X. How do you go about it?

A Find out who is in charge of your area of interest and write to him or her well in advance of your visit. Suggest what you might do for Company X. If the response is positive, set up a precise appointment before leaving home.

B Step in at Company X's office during the course of your visit and ask to see the president.

C Call a day or two in advance and make a date to visit with anyone who's around.

Comments

A is best. As Americans hate to waste time, they're not apt to see you unless they have good reason to believe it's worthwhile. You can chance *C* sometimes, but your odds are poor of seeing anyone consequential. *B* is fairly hopeless, although out of politeness some minor functionary may see you. As a person with demonstrated time to spend in waiting, you will be assumed to be of little importance.

SITUATION 7

You hire a nanny. Although you consider her wages very high, you are glad to have her as she is sensible and reliable. However, it distresses you that she calls you by your first name. You don't want to hurt her feelings, but you wish she would call you Mrs. Ayashi. Can you ask her to?

A No. She would be too insulted at the suggestion. She hasn't called anyone by title since her schooldays.

B Yes, but you must ask tactfully.

C Yes, just tell her you think it is very rude of her to call you by first name.

Comments

B. Tact should spare you hurt feelings. You might bring up the subject at a happy moment when you are offering some kind of treat so that she will realize that you bear her no ill will personally.

If she is a mature woman, we assume that you have taken care to call her Mrs. Eliot, rather than Rose. You should explain to her that in your country only people who have known each other for a very long time are on first name terms, and while you hold her in high regard, you cannot get used to the sound of your given name coming from someone you met so recently. You might add that you know this is not the custom in the USA and you understand that she does not mean to be rude. If she is a great deal younger than you, you may call her by first name while explaining that where you come from younger people always address older ones by title.

CULTURE TIPS A–Z

Bargaining Almost the only chances you get to bargain in the USA are when buying houses and cars.

Black The color of mourning.

Currency As bills are all green and of the same size, foreigners easily mix up American money. Pennies, nickels, dimes, and quarters are worth 1 cent, 5 cents, 10 cents, and 25 cents respectively. You will have to study them to know which is which.

Envelopes How to address:

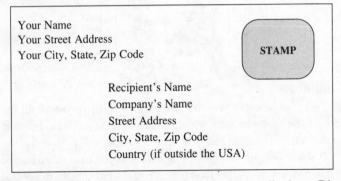

Your Name
Your Street Address
Your City, State, Zip Code

STAMP

Recipient's Name
Company's Name
Street Address
City, State, Zip Code
Country (if outside the USA)

Firemen Paid by taxes, not by the person who calls them. Ditto police.

Floor levels The street-level (ground) floor is called the first floor. Go up one flight of stairs and you're on the second floor.

Hitchhiking. Don't do it; it's not safe. And don't pick up hitchhikers either.

Modesty Crops up in strange places. People do not change into bathing suits on beaches, even hiding underneath a towel.

Rent The advertised price of an apartment is for the monthly rental. The renter is expected to mail or deliver a check just before the first of each month. Upon first renting an apartment, one nearly always must deposit an extra month's rent and a cleaning fee (about $100). Both are returned to you when you leave.

Sales tax A percentage added to the price of most goods sold and collected by state and/or local governments. Amount varies, but is usually 6–8%. The advertised price is without sales tax.

Shaving Most American women shave hair from their underarms and from their lower legs (below the knees).

Shoes You don't take them off when you enter a house. But don't put your feet on the furniture.

Shopping If many people are waiting to be served, they form an invisible line (queue), in which each person knows his/her place. You must keep track of who came ahead of you and who came behind so that you will know when it is your turn. When the person behind the counter says, "Who's next?", you do not push in ahead of turn.

Sneezing Someone may say "God bless you," or "Gesundheit" when you sneeze. It's an old custom to keep the vital force within you from escaping.

Stamps Buy them at post offices, which all fly US flags. Postal boxes are blue.

Store hours Vary widely. Some department stores are open 10 a.m. to 9 p.m. every weekday, closing at 6 p.m. on weekends. Others normally close at 6:30 p.m., except on Thursdays, when they stay open until 9 p.m. Some supermarkets are open 24 hours a day. Many drugstores close at 9 p.m., others at midnight. In some communities, everything closes early. Smaller specialty stores may be closed on Sundays, especially if they are located in business districts.

Superstitions Numerous among Americans, but not taken very seriously. Bad luck comes from walking under ladders, the number 13, black cats, and broken mirrors. Good luck is contained in rabbit's feet, four-leaf clovers, and knocking on wood. Friday the 13th is considered a very unlucky day, and some people will not take an airplane on that day.

Teeth Thanks to all that sugar, Americans have many cavities, but luckily we have good dentists and fluoride added to the water is lowering the rate of dental decay. A large number of American children have their teeth straightened with braces at considerable cost to their parents.

Time Continental USA has four time zones. The East Coast is three hours ahead of the West Coast.

Tipping In restaurants, the standard tip is 15%, although for first-rate service in a grand place, you could make it 20%.

Bartenders and cocktail waitresses usually get 10%.

Hairdressers are tipped 10–20%. The shampoo person gets $1.

Cloakroom attendants get $1 per coat.

Taxi drivers expect a 10–15% tip.

Bell-boys: About $1 per item for taking luggage to rooms.

Chambermaids: After several days in a hotel, leave $2.

Doormen: 50 cents to $1 for hailing a cab.

Parking valet: $1 for bringing your car.

X The symbol of a kiss, which you might use in signing a letter. Also used by teachers to indicate an answer is wrong.

Yawns Should be stifled in company as yawns indicate boredom, but if you must yawn, cover your mouth.

BIBLIOGRAPHY

The following recommendations include only those books that I feel would be most helpful to foreigners trying to understand Americans and their way of life. It is, of course, far from a complete reading list.

American Cultural Patterns. Edward C. Stewart, Intercultural Press, 1972. An excellent study of American beliefs and behavior.

American Values. Ralph H. Gabriel, Greenwood Press, 1974. An in-depth study.

American Ways. Gary Althen, Intercultural Press, 1988. A basic, easy-to-read review of American attitudes by a foreign student advisor.

Class. Paul Fussell, Ballantine Books, 1983. Not only does Fussell insist that America has a class system, he describes in minute detail the elements that separate the strata. A most amusing book and thoroughly practical for anyone who seriously wishes to rise socially.

Coping with America. Peter Trudgill, Basil Blackwell Inc., 1985. A charming and practical book for the traveller by an Englishman. Mr. Trudgill is amused by Americans, but affectionate. His observant eye notes many baffling and subtle details.

Cultural Literacy: What Every American Needs to Know. E.D. Hirsch, Jr., Vintage Books, 1988. Hirsch laments the loss of basic cultural knowledge among American children. The appendix consists of a list of the terms a literate American should recognize.

Cultural Misunderstandings. Raymonde Carroll. The University Chicago Press, 1988. If you're just going to read one book on cultural differences, this is the one (especially if you have married into another culture). Compares French and Americans, but the points are universal.

The Dance of Life. Edward T. Hall, Anchor Books/Doubleday, 1983. An anthropologist explains why time is perceived so differently in various cultures and why Americans go by the clock.

The Decline of Pleasure. Walter Kerr, Simon & Schuster, 1962. A wry look at the American refusal to relax and enjoy life.

Democracy in America. Alexis de Tocqueville, Vintage Books, 1945 (first published in 1835). De Tocqueville wrote about the uniqueness of America, and many of his observations remain apt today.

Domestic Manners of the Americans. Fanny Trollope, Oxford University Press, 1984 (first published in 1832). Mrs. Trollope, a lively writer, found Americans ignorant and parties dull, but she grants that the USA was a fine country to get ahead in.

The Economist Business Traveller's Guides: United States. Prentice-Hall, 1987. A stylishly written book with loads of information – from industry analysis to names of hotels and restaurants in major cities.

Future Shock. Alvin Toffler, Random House, 1970. Describes how a fast-changing world affects personal stability and communities.

Host Family Survival Kit. Nancy King and Ken Huff, Intercultural Press, 1985. A guide for Americans who are sheltering exchange students, but equally useful in helping the students understand the hosts. Includes a good description of the culture shock process.

In Search of Self: Toward a Cross-Cultural Psychology. Alan Roland, Princeton University Press, 1988. A psychoanalyst who worked with American, Japanese, and Indian patients discovers very basic differences in family attachments.

Living in the USA. Alison R. Lanier, Intercultural Press, 1988. Much practical information, such as how to buy a car, send a telegram, rent an apartment, and find a bathroom.

Lost in Translation. Eva Hoffman, Penguin Books, 1989. A beautifully written account of life in America by a Polish-born refugee.

More Like US. James Fallows, Houghton Mifflin, 1989. A book dedicated to stopping America's drift towards a rigid, class-bound system. Fallows believes the USA is losing the mobility that once made it great.

People of Plenty: Economic Abundance and The American Character. David M. Potter, University of Chicago Press, 1954. Recognizes how much of American behavior is simply an outgrowth of affluence.

A People's History of the United States. Howard Zinn, Harper & Row, 1981. About the people history books usually ignore and what their lives were really like.

Two Years in the Melting Pot. Liu Zongren, China Books, 1988. Anyone suffering culture shock will find solace reading of Liu's distress in America.

INDEX